DEVELOPING
PROPHETIC
CULTURE

BUILDING HEALTHY CHURCHES
THAT HEAR JESUS CLEARLY

Phil Wilthew

malcolm down
PUBLISHING

First published 2016 by Malcolm Down Publishing Ltd.
www.malcolmdown.co.uk

British Library Cataloguing in Publication Data
A catalogue record for this book is available from the British Library.

ISBN 978-1-910786-47-5

Cover design by Toby Cosh

Printed in the UK by Bell & Bain Ltd, Glasgow.

What Others Are Saying About
Developing Prophetic Culture

Developing Prophetic Culture by Phil Wilthew is a much needed resource for the Church at this time. The prophetic is often marginalised by fears of weirdness, eccentricity and fringe theology. This unhelpful caricature is totally dispelled by an excellent biblical overview of the place of the prophetic in biblical history and how that relates to us in the contemporary church. There are quotes from sources with a rich theological background, and combined with Phil's grasp of Scripture, and his hands-on practical experience, this book is a must read for every church leader, and anyone who is keen to understand the place of the prophetic in church life.

Covering personal issues like hearing God, character, courage, anointing and the more corporate issues such as prophecy in the church meeting, the practical teaching will equip any believer and church to grow in understanding that God is a speaking God.

He also demonstrates the bigger picture that prophecy has a kingdom dimension, speaking into the lives of unbelievers and into secular culture. His writing style is direct and uncomplicated, and rich in personal illustration.

This book is a must read, and is the best equipping book on this subject I have encountered so far.

Dave Fellingham, Author of Worship Restored, Songwriter & Musician. Based at King's Church, Horsham

I thank God for the gift that Phil Wilthew is to the Body of Christ! I have known him for over 10 years and we have journeyed together through the maze that is the prophetic. In this book,

Phil unpacks his journey into the prophetic, creating prophetic communities and empowering believers to live out their destiny. He does so with raw honesty and insightful revelation, grounded in a strong understanding of our sonship. His emphasis on discovering the prophetic through the lens of kingdom influence is so helpful in taking what has been essentially a 'church thing' and unlocking the power of sonship, mission, and influencing the world around us. With practical tools and significant wisdom, Phil takes the reader through a journey of discovery into the prophetic, even if they do not feel 'called' to be a prophet. Phil has lived this message in his family, his church and community. He is doing what he has written in these pages. Movement leaders, church pastors and congregants alike need to read this book because it is a blueprint for an emerging prophetic wineskin that is filled with hope, joy and a revelation of a good Father! It will unlock your church to see itself as the prophetic community it is and God's preferred method to change the world. Read it, it will do you good!

Julian Adams, Author of *Gaining Heaven's Perspective* and *Kiss of the Father*, Prophet and Teacher based in Durban, South Africa

Having been a Christian now for over 35 years, and a full-time pastor for the last 10 of those years, I can honestly say the last three years have been the most amazing. There was a radical shift in my heart, my mind and my thinking due, in no small part, to Phil Wilthew and the team at King's Arms.

I had realised, early in 2013, that I was ambitious for God, I was ambitious for His church, I was ambitious for church growth, I was even ambitious for the supernatural but I was not really hungry for Him! Ambition, I have discovered, is not the same as hunger for God Himself. Part of my journey took me later in 2013 to a Father Heart Conference at King's Arms. It was at that conference that Phil Wilthew made a statement that really offended me, was possibly heretical in my eyes and so angered me that if I was closer I would have happily punched him! He said that *God's ultimate purpose in sending Jesus was not the remittance of sins but the adoption of sons.* In that moment, and the ones that followed, I was offended into an amazing revelation that has radically changed me, changed my life, my ministry and ultimately how I see church! (Phil unpacks that statement in Chapter 2 of his book.)

Since then I have got to know Phil and the team at King's Arms, and now count him as a personal friend. The man you get to know in this book is the man himself. Authentic, prophetic, radical, practical and real. He is the real deal! He is not only a tried and tested prophet but is an incredible leader who not only impacts the people he comes into contact with but changes atmospheres and shapes cultures too. I have no hesitation in commending *Developing Prophetic Culture* because I commend the man!

This book will impact you and, if you allow it, you will be led into incredible revelation.

It clearly and concisely takes you on a journey of understanding, revelation and practical application in the prophetic, making it accessible to everyone.

If you are a church leader, hungry for more of the prophetic in your church, if you want to see prophets raised and released where you are, and a prophetic culture established, then this is the book for you.

This book is not only for church leaders but for anyone who wants to hear Jesus more clearly. Whoever you are, this book will

change you and train you, allowing you to develop a prophetic culture wherever you are – at church, at work, school, college, home, the school gate or the coffee shops you frequent.
Andy Robinson, Eldership Team Leader, King's Church, Horsham

Are you wondering about the prophetic? Are you prophetic? Are you interested in how this gifting affects the Church today? If you have any of these questions, you will find answers that will help you discover how the prophetic applies to you and your church. Phil Wilthew has given us some wonderful information, practical application and guidelines for moulding the world of the prophetic. Not only is the information going to be a value to you but you can rest assured that he and the team he works with at King's Arms are walking in the values that he has shared. As we have travelled to bodies around the world, we have not found a purer expression of people whose desire is to please the Lord than we have at King's Arms. Phil is an amazing example of the prophetic ministry working in team in the Church.
Tom & Suzie Brock, Wave of Life Ministries, California

I have appreciated and been blessed for many years by Phil Wilthew's prophetic gift. Now, in this excellent new book, he refreshingly sets prophetic ministry in the contexts of our sonship, community and a broad biblical view of the Kingdom of God. It is also full of practical and wise application, for example, for handling the prophetic in our corporate gatherings. I am very happy to commend *Developing Prophetic Culture* to you.
David Devenish, International Church Planter, Author and Leader within the Newfrontiers family of churches

Phil paints a beautiful picture of how intentionally creating a prophetic culture enables Kingdom life to flow into and through individual believers and gathered churches. His book is a provocation to not settle for what we already know of the prophetic, but to believe God for the more we read about in Scripture. I believe if we really 'get this' as churches, we will see an increased outpouring of the Holy Spirit's presence and power as we gather together, leading to an increased impact on the world around us. Phil lives what he writes and I have the privilege of seeing the fruit of that first hand. Read his book and be inspired and equipped to hear Jesus clearly.

Wendy Mann, Author of *Naturally Supernatural* and Leader of Training for Supernatural Ministry School, Bedford, UK

Phil's heart for empowering people in the prophetic shines through the text. I heartily endorse the way he writes about overpowering exclusivity, an 'everyone has' approach and his determination to 'make space for others to shine'. This is a helpful book for those who are 'eagerly desiring to prophesy' as well as a useful tool for leaders. It is surely time for prophetic gifts to be released in their fullness and for those who lead to be prepared for some messy moments. Phil helps us to see the need to be hearing 'prophecy which comes out of a future perspective', to 'speak words that release life not death' and to grow in our understanding of the ways in which God can speak. Mindful of some of the more difficult words I've had to bring over the years, I particularly like the comment that 'it should be a red flag for leaders if they are only ever hearing the things they want to hear'! A very useful and provocative read!

Ginny Burgin, Prophetess within Newfrontiers family of churches, based in Sheffield, UK

One of the greatest achievements we can make is to create around ourselves environments that enrich the lives of others. In this book Phil very helpfully outlines some of the principles and practicalities of creating a prophetic culture in a church. Using biblical principles and personal experience, he takes us on a journey of discovery into such realms. Having worked hard at Eastgate to develop such a culture, and having known Phil and his church for many years, I found this book to be a helpful and inspiring tool that can equip individuals and churches. I recommend this book to you and suggest that it would be a good book to study together in groups, so that the journey can be enjoyed with others and prophetic cultures created.

Dr Pete Carter, Director of Eastgate, Medical Doctor and author of *Unwrapping Lazarus*

Acknowledgements

There are so many people that I want to thank for shaping both the content of this book and myself.

Thank you Mum and Dad for your constant example of faithfulness and love for Jesus that continues to inspire me today. You created a family environment where I learned to know God. Thank you for passing on a godly inheritance and for making prophetic legacy possible.

Thank you to my church family who have played a huge part in my own wholeness and joy. There is no culture quite like the King's Arms culture and I love you so much. The best is yet to come. Special thanks to my prophetic friends, from whom I have learned so much and with whom I am honoured to serve alongside. Thank you to my fellow elders: Simon, Steve, Paul and Roydon. I am humbled to work with such gifted and kind friends. Thanks for pulling the best out of me.

Thank you to the men who have modelled a passion for the presence of God and the prophetic through the years, in a way that has greatly shaped who I have become. Thank you to Terry Virgo, David Fellingham, Kris Vallotton, Julian Adams and Simon Holley. I am so grateful to God for each of you.

Special thanks to Dad for the hours of editing and support you have given on this manuscript. I could not have done it without you. Your insights and eye for detail have been invaluable. Thank you to Hannah, Toby, Malcolm and Sarah for your help in putting this book together. Thanks, too, for the countless people who have encouraged me to keep going and actually write it!

Thank you to my amazing kids, Lauren and Sam. Being a dad has been the greatest privilege of my life. I am so proud of you both. You were born to change the world and I'm right behind you!

Lastly, thank you to my wife Carole. You are more courageous and special than anyone realises. I always said you were the most amazing woman I had ever met and that is as true today as ever before. You are God's precious gift to me and I love you with all of my heart. Thanks for believing in me. There is so much more to come!

Dedication

This book is dedicated to my good friend Bob Holloway, my prophetic father in the Lord. You taught me to hear and I will be eternally grateful. Thank you.

Contents

Foreword

I count it a privilege to have had Phil Wilthew as a colleague and friend for many years. I'm so excited to see the release of this book, which is the product of a life lived pursuing Jesus and working alongside him to build His Church and extend His Kingdom.

Phil has the rare ability to not only carry an outstanding prophetic gift but the skill to use that gift to build and strengthen whilst equipping and releasing others to do the same. It's one thing to prophesy; entirely another to raise up other prophets and to develop a prophetic community. Phil has helped to do this with us and he does it with winsome humour, real life stories and provoking comments that result in people around him being encouraged yet aspiring for more.

What's more Phil lives it in his life. His stories are not all from 'days gone by' but from yesterday or last week, and the way that he leads his family through joy-filled and tear-filled seasons gives such honour to God. It's been a privilege to walk with Phil, pray with Phil and talk through the big issues of life and ministry with Phil, and I and many others around him are richer for his life and friendship.

I believe Phil to be a true prophet and we recognise him as such in our local community and the network of churches to which we belong. You will be greatly blessed as you receive from him through the pages of this book.

Simon Holley
Lead Elder, King's Arms Church, Bedford

Introduction:
Doughnuts and a Date with Destiny
Discovering a Prophetic Culture

Sometimes you don't know what you are looking for until you find it, and then it becomes a non negotiable in your life. That was my experience in 1994 on discovering what I now realise was a prophetic culture in the King's Arms Church, Bedford.

I had visited Bedford some years before as an eighteen-year-old, just before embarking on a gap year in the United States. During two weeks' theological training, one evening my friends and I went along to the relatively new King's Arms, which sounded like a pub but was actually a church, meeting in a local school hall. The church was already renowned for two things: a radical heart for the poor and its tasty doughnuts, which were served up in a half-time meeting break. I was impressed by both and ate far too many doughnuts. As the meeting resumed a team of four from the church stood at the front and began to pick people out to prophesy over them. I had never seen this before and was even more amazed when I was asked to stand.

The team began to prophesy over me: 'The word for you is Solomon. You are to build on your father's heritage. You are a man of quality and wisdom, a "master builder" as in 2 Chronicles 6. God will be pleased to inhabit your dwelling and everything that you build.'

Wow! It was a life-defining moment. I still have goose bumps just remembering. Not only had I encountered God powerfully, I had also encountered an embryonic prophetic culture which, twelve years later, I rediscovered as I moved to be part of the church.

On occasions God imparts something to your spirit that takes your mind years to catch up with. In a moment, He can drop keys into your soul designed to unlock doors many years into your future. This was such a moment for me. God had shown me a small glimpse of what a prophetic culture actually looks like – how it feels and smells, and this started me on a journey of discovery still going on to this day.

This book is born out of a passion for Jesus and His desire to awaken and unleash churches that are fully able to hear His voice and communicate it to others. This, essentially, is what prophecy is. Hearing from God and passing it on. Simple!

Hearing His voice is what each of us was made for. Hearing His voice is what first irresistibly drew us into the arms of God's grace, as He brought us from death to life in a heartbeat. Listening to His voice is what literally makes our souls live (Isaiah 55:3). Being able to distinguish the Shepherd's voice is what marks us out as His people, the Sheep of His pasture (John 10:4-5). Hearing Him is like eating daily bread which feeds the deepest needs of our spirit (Matthew 4:4).

It is for this reason that the apostle Paul says we should eagerly desire prophecy above all other gifts, because it strengthens and builds up the Church (1 Corinthians 14:12). When we hear God accurately, we become strong. The Greek word translated 'build up' literally means 'to build a home that is a suitable dwelling place'. In other words, the prophetic, when functioning properly, should result in the creation of an environment where God is pleased to dwell; where He feels at home among His people.

Through the years I have seen many churches with a high value for prophecy but a perceptibly low understanding of how to build cultures that enable the prophetic to flourish. We love the gift, but are unsure how to build an environment in which this gift can thrive, not just survive.

I am no gardener. In fact, that is a huge understatement. I

remember my mum trying to teach me the names of various plants and flowers when I was younger, but to no avail. I was a hopeless case and forgot instantly the difference between a hydrangea and a hyacinth. However, I did learn and still understand the importance of atmosphere and environment when it comes to the health of a flower or plant. In particular, I learnt that mothers get cross when sons kick their football repeatedly in to the flowerbeds. Sorry Mum!

Environment matters hugely to the way living things develop and grow, including people. This is one of the key messages in the Parable of the Sower (Mathew 13:1-8), which Jesus told to demonstrate how different soil (heart) conditions impact the growth rate of the seed (Kingdom). It is sobering to realise that God's all-powerful and living words can be so affected by the culture or environment into which they are sown.

Creating a prophetic culture has everything to do with how we develop the right conditions for prophets and prophetic gifting to flourish across the whole church community, from the young to the old and from new believer to mature believer.

I believe the reason not many of us have ever experienced Paul's description of biblical prophetic ministry, where guests among us have the secrets of their hearts revealed, crying, 'God is really among you!' (1 Corinthians 14:24-25), is because we have not paid attention to the issue of prophetic culture in our churches. We have reduced and relegated prophecy and, as a result, assigned it to the realms of sweet thoughts and flower pictures, rather than the spiritual dynamite God intended it to be for his people.

Culture creation has its roots in the agricultural world as farmers cultivated their land to grow certain crops and not others. Building a prophetic culture is about creating the right spiritual ecosystem, one where hearing Jesus' voice powerfully and clearly becomes the new normal.

The key questions for us in this book are: How can we create the kind of culture that enables powerful, Jesus-honouring, Bible-believing prophetic ministry to function as it should? What would this prophetic culture look like in our churches, families and lives; and how can we build it?

My hope, as you read this book, is that the Holy Spirit inspires and enables you to create fertile prophetic environments through which Jesus is made famous and the Father's Kingdom is unleashed into the world around us.

It is time for a new prophetic revolution.

Phil Wilthew

Chapter One:
New Creation Reality
Rediscovering the Lenses of Kingdom Culture

Jesus is Alive!

My own journey in hearing God started at the tender age of nine in what I can only describe as one of THE mountaintop moments of my life, where everything changed. At the time, my dad was a Baptist pastor and I had grown up in a happy and secure Christian family and had given my life to Christ at the tender age of six. Yet despite this, I had little or no framework for what I was about to experience one night as we travelled to hear a well-known healing evangelist speak at a meeting in Sussex, close to where we lived.

Two things still stand out vividly about that evening. First, his graphic portrayal of Christ on the cross, as he preached the gospel, which set off the two elderly ladies in front of me in a fit of complaints at his blood-soaked powers of description. 'Ooooo, that's disgusting,' one lady said to the other.

'Unnecessary!' replied the other. Secondly, I remember him transitioning to an astonishing outpouring of words of knowledge and miracles. I sat dumbfounded as he called out different people's exact physical condition and circumstances and then saw one after another instantly healed. I was captured!

I watched him pray for one man whose legs were different lengths by several inches, which was notable by the huge raised shoe he had just taken off and set beside his chair. As he prayed, the shorter leg shot out to match the other, causing a visible gasp from those looking on. I rubbed my eyes in disbelief; it was as if

21

a cartoon had come to life in front of me. To this day, it is still one of the most dramatic instantaneous miracles I have ever seen first-hand as God, in a moment, effortlessly inserted new bone, sinews, muscles and ligaments. I could hardly believe what I was seeing and experiencing.

This God, who I believed in yet had never really encountered, was, well, actually alive! He was doing stuff! Cue even more stunned silence, when he picked me out, had a word of knowledge about my poor sleep (which was very poor) and he prayed for me. Overwhelmed with the whole occasion I burst into tears and knew I would never be the same again. God had encountered me. As we stepped back into our house that night I was beaming ear to ear and could not stop saying to my parents, 'He's alive! Jesus is actually alive!'

When you experience the Kingdom, you encounter the King. His Kingdom is alive, because He is alive. This is a revelation the world is waiting for.

What awakened my soul to the wonder of hearing His voice that night? It was being in an atmosphere where the Kingdom of God was both declared and demonstrated. Kingdom culture is the only umbrella under which hearing His voice truly flourishes. If we are to create vibrant prophetic centres we must rediscover our theology and love for the Kingdom.

I wonder, when people encounter my life or the church family, do they encounter a God who is alive and on display in that same way? Do they run back to their homes, as I did that day, exclaiming 'Jesus is alive! Jesus is alive!' because they should! When the Kingdom of God becomes the central lens through which we live and see the world, Jesus is demonstrated in all His Technicolor, risen glory, because Kingdom is all about announcing His rule and His reign. Jesus is Lord!

When the Bible uses the word 'Kingdom', it speaks of the realm or rule of a King, and is used differently to a word like 'Church', which means those called out by God. George Eldon Ladd puts the difference this way: 'The Kingdom is the rule of God; the Church is the society of men.'[1] In other words, all of the Church is in the Kingdom, but not all of the Kingdom is in the Church. God's desire, as we shall see, is not just to fill His people, but to fill the entire cosmos. God has not come to play on the margins; He has come to redeem the planet. We have been called out of the world (the Church) so that we can transform the world (the Kingdom)!

Jesus' Central Message

It is no surprise, then, that the Kingdom of God was Jesus' central message and the dominant theme of His teaching. With over one hundred references to the Kingdom in the first three gospels alone, we build a picture of Jesus' primary prophetic perspective. The start of both John the Baptist's and Jesus' ministries began with the same, unifying clarion call: 'Repent' (meaning change the way you think), 'for the kingdom of heaven has come near' (Matthew 3:2).

In other words, in order to live (and prophesy) accurately, we have to think accurately. The Kingdom is waiting to break out, therefore I need to start thinking like a King's Kid! Repentance is not primarily sinful remorse, but saintly reformation. As I begin to reform my thinking to look and sound like Jesus, I am able to participate in all that the King wants to do on this planet and in my life. The apostle Paul, writing to the Romans, spells this truth out brilliantly:

'Do not conform to the pattern of this world, but be transformed by the renewing of your mind. Then you will be able to test and approve what God's will is – his good, pleasing and perfect will.' (Romans 12:2)

When our minds (our beliefs and understanding) begin to get re-set according to His Kingdom values, we re-present Him more accurately to the world. Perhaps this is why Jesus also used his final 40 post-resurrection days speaking about the Kingdom of God (Acts 1:3) to His own disciples, precisely because He knew this was the big idea! For a world to be reformed, His people must first be transformed through Kingdom logic, not worldly wisdom. It is only in 'the Kingdom' that disciples will be able to understand their real identity and mighty mission.

Rooting our prophetic gifting into an understanding of the Kingdom is critical to make sure it is big enough, bold enough and broad enough to actually impact nations and change hearts. Prophecy is a Kingdom weapon, designed to extend God's rule and reign, not just in the Church, but in the very fabric of our society.

The whole of the New Testament screams loudly and clearly that the Kingdom of God is the central message and that this worldview should dominate our thinking, our teaching, our living and our prophesying!

Yet, nowhere is the Kingdom explicitly described or explained. There is no easy one-word biblical definition to pull off the shelf. So how do we go about understanding the Kingdom and lay this as the foundational worldview in our churches and lives?

The Kingdom in Historical Context
None of us like being quoted out of context, yet we do this with the words of Jesus. Context brings meaning. When Jesus came preaching about the Kingdom He did so in a certain historical and cultural context that brought meaning to the words He taught, at that time.

If I were jump in my time machine, teleport back to the days of Queen Victoria and try to tell her about microchips and mobile phones, my words would mean little in the context of her world, where lavatories were only just being invented. Likewise, Jesus' teaching on the Kingdom will mean little in the 21st century unless we get into the mindset of a first-century Jewish man or woman, for whom the phrase 'Kingdom of God' came laden with meaning, longing and expectation.

The Great Hope

Jesus taught Jewish hearers who believed that history was divided into two ages or eras. First, they believed in this present age, which was characterised by imperfections, suffering, pain and trials. For a nation whose glory-days had long been lost and who were now an occupied state, these realities were difficult to miss. Life was hard.

However, the great Jewish, and indeed biblical hope, was in a second age to come, which was characterised by restoration, vindication, justice, peace, healing and everlasting comfort. From their reading of the great prophets Isaiah and Daniel, they understood that this second age, or Kingdom, would come when God's Messiah would win a great victory over sin and darkness, usher in a new day and bring about the redemption, not just of this world, but of all creation. His coming would see the lame walk, the deaf hear and mute tongues shout for joy. The great hope was that God's coming Kingdom would swallow up the pain and torment of this present age.

For centuries, the great Jewish longing was for the unveiling of the Messiah who would bring the Kingdom. As the days of Jesus approach, the nation is weary of waiting but still pregnant with longing for the King and His Kingdom.

It is little wonder, then, that whole towns empty to visit the locust-eating, camel-coat wearing John the Baptist, who begins to announce 'The Kingdom is here – one is coming who will baptise you with spirit and fire!' John prophesies that the second age, the Kingdom of God, is about to begin and that Messiah is on the doorstep of history! As Jesus approaches him one day to be baptised, John declares – 'This is the one!'

Jesus also adds to this growing fervour in the nation by announcing the arrival of the Kingdom. In His home-town synagogue of Nazareth, He stands and reads the words of their favourite kingdom-prophet, Isaiah, back to them, quoting: 'The Spirit of the Lord is upon me, because he has anointed me to proclaim good news to the poor. He has sent me to proclaim freedom for the prisoners and recovery of sight to the blind, to set the oppressed free, to proclaim the year of the Lord's favour' (Luke 4:16-19).

Luke tells us that as He gave the scroll back to the attendant and sat down, the eyes of everyone in the synagogue were fastened on Him. In a scene tense with drama and filled with intrigue, He announces, 'Today, this scripture is fulfilled in your hearing' (Luke 4:20-21).

Oh my! What a moment! Oh to have been a fly on the wall to see the faces of those listening to Jesus as He clearly tells them – 'What you have been waiting for all these centuries is now here. I am the one and the second age has begun!'

The Invasion of the Future

What happens in Jesus was completely supernatural, unexpected and out-of-the-box. Through Jesus' life and ministry – in His miracles, healings, authority, crucifixion, death, resurrection, ascension and giving of the Spirit – the future world Isaiah and Daniel had prophesied arrives in advance and breaks into present history. Suddenly, the powers of the end of the world had arrived early.

Everything that should happen at the end of history, in the second age, suddenly arrived before time in Jesus. The future has now broken into the present creating an altogether new dimension; before this world has come to a close the future world has already begun.

Two eras have been merged into one. We live in the presence

of the future! We live in a world that still faces the imperfections and pain of this present age, but simultaneously lives in the age of God's Kingdom, where His future world of healing, wholeness, restoration and joy is breaking in.

Jesus has inaugurated the rule of God (Kingdom) on the planet and this is characterised by peace, justice, wholeness, comfort, healing and salvation; not just in the sweet by-and-by, but also in the here and now. And this Kingdom is entrusted to believers who now dispense what Christ has won.

Prophesying the Kingdom

One of the implications of this truth about the Kingdom is that our prophesying now happens from the perspective of future, not just present, reality. We prophesy with the knowledge that Jesus has finished His victorious work on the cross, and that the empty tomb invites us to expect and hope for much. The era of the gloomy prophet who looks as if he has been sucking lemons, is over. We prophesy from victory. We prophesy from hope. We prophesy from the future to the present. Prophesying is partaking in the inaugurated rule and reign of God, through Christ, as we dispense His life to others.

This is why Paul says that prophecy always encourages, strengthens and comforts (1 Corinthians 14:3). He understood that a new creation prophetic perspective always transmits good news, because this is what the King and His Kingdom is like! When we prophesy, we dispense the victory that Jesus has already secured.

With this as our backdrop, here are some of the practical implications of prophesying through a Kingdom perspective.

a. We Prophesy the Increase of His Kingdom, Not the Church

It is vital we have a passion for the Church, but we must understand that the Church sits under the umbrella of something

27

bigger – God is ruling the cosmos and His rule is extending on the earth through His people.

Therefore, Kingdom prophets understand that God's intent is not just the restoration of the Church but the reformation of society. Our perspective is global not parochial. God's heart is for His kingdom to shape and define business, arts, media and government just as much as your Bible week or leaders' weekend away. God plans to rule over everything.

The trend in Western Christianity to label things as 'gospel-shaped' and 'gospel-centred' is brilliant, as long as we remember that the gospel Jesus taught was not just about the conversion of the soul, but the gospel of the Kingdom which is God's rule over everything! If the earth is the Lord's and everything in it, the gospel we preach had better be big enough to include His plan to fill the whole cosmos with His glory.

In recent years it has been such a pleasure to see the prophetic bringing the Kingdom into other spheres of culture and society. Recently, I prophesied over a man in another part of the world, that he would be raised up to be a prophetic voice to rulers in his nation and begin to speak words of life. Within just a few weeks he had a series of four dreams in which he saw himself prophesying over the vice-president of the country. With no idea yet of what God wanted to say, he began to pray that God would open up an opportunity. Quite by chance, he met the daughter of the vice-president and, in less than a year, he found himself in the VP's office prophesying words of hope and life that will have great significance in that land.

One verse prior to Paul's teaching on God giving the Church apostles and prophets to equip and train, he reminds the Ephesians that God's goal was always to fill the whole universe through the ascended Christ (Ephesians 4:10-11). Commenting on this truth, Peter O'Brien says:

'Having achieved dominion over all the powers through

his victorious ascent, he sovereignly distributes gifts to the members of his body. The building of the body is inextricably linked with his intention of filling the universe with his rule, since the church is his instrument in carrying out his purposes for the cosmos.'[2]

God's goal is to fill the whole cosmos with the knowledge of His presence and rule. Your prophetic job description just got a whole lot bigger! A prophet's perspective is not just to make the Church ready, but to join Christ in transforming the cosmos with His rule and reign. A Kingdom mindset forces us to think beyond the Church and into the marketplace. George MacLeod puts this brilliantly when he says:

'I simply argue that the cross be raised again at the center of the market place as well as on the steeple of the church. I am recovering the claim that Jesus was not crucified in a cathedral between two candles, but on a cross between two thieves; on a town garbage heap; on a cross- roads so cosmopolitan that they had to write his title in Hebrew and Latin and Greek; at the kind of place where cynics talk smut, and thieves curse, and soldiers gamble. Because that is where he died and that is what he died about. And that is where Christians should be and what Christians should be about.'[3]

b. We Prophesy the Message and Secrets of the Kingdom

In Matthew 13:11 we read of Jesus, 'And he answered them, "To you it has been given to know the secrets of the kingdom of heaven, but to them it has not been given"' (NRSV).

The word the Greek New Testament uses here for 'secret' is *mysterion*, which, as you can guess, means a mystery. Elsewhere, Jesus calls these mysteries 'the keys of the kingdom of heaven' (Matthew 16:19). Something has been entrusted to God's people that is not common knowledge. The Kingdom doesn't work from the point of view of education or titles, but from revelation and relationship.

One of the things Kingdom prophecy does is bring God's people back to the Kingdom secrets that really matter and reminds them to use the divine keys which will unlock eternal destinies and impossible circumstances.

One example of a Kingdom secret is that to see and inherit the Kingdom you have to become like a little child (Luke 18:16; Matthew 18:3). Childlikeness is not a commonly taught value system in the world in which we live, yet this is one of the mysterious keys that enables the Kingdom to come.

One cause of great celebration in our church has been to see children demonstrating the Kingdom effortlessly as they simply believe what God says. A few weeks ago, our 8- to 10-year-olds came into the end of our Sunday morning meeting to lead a time of prophetic ministry, calling out various words of knowledge. Two children had combined their words together as they asked if there was a lady in the room with a pink top and a green cast on her right ankle. Now, that's pretty specific! Sure enough, a lady came forward matching these exact descriptions and received prayer from the kids. A month later, as she had her cast removed, the doctors were amazed to find a leg that was already strong and ready to be walked on ahead of time.

Our prophetic ministry exists to remind people of these hidden Kingdom truths and it call God's people to a timely use of them.

c. We Prophesy with Love and Faith, Understanding Kingdom Tension
Jesus taught that the Kingdom was simultaneously a future reality, a present reality, a near reality and a delayed reality. That's a lot of realities! That's back to the future on steroids!

Unless you understand that you live in the presence of two ages, you will never understand the glory and the frustration of the Christian life. For prophetic people, whose internal spiritual clocks are hardwired into the future, this is especially important. Prophetic people typically live with a great sense of restlessness about the present because they are hearing God about the future. This is how their gift helps bring us into God-initiated change. The prophetic is often anachronistic, living outside of its current time zone, somewhere into the future, pulling down God's plans into the here and now and creating a sense of faith to engage with God's promises. As a result, prophetic people can sometimes come across as, how shall I put it, rather discontent!

This came home to me at a staff review when a colleague asked: 'How content to do you feel?' I scored my contentment fairly low, which had nothing to do with my marriage, family life or satisfaction at work. This alarmed him considerably, until I explained how the prophetic often works in creating a longing for the future. When you live in the midst of two ages, one passing and one eternal, navigating the tension this creates is critical.

You are not called to get depressed or give in to the frustrations of the present. Neither are you to be triumphalistic or passive about pulling the future into the now. Kingdom prophets are called to bring heaven to earth. Understanding that we do not see all that we want to now, we must nevertheless keep believing and prophesying for more.

The Kingdom has come and is coming. It is here and it has not yet arrived. We are living paradoxes. I cannot put it any better than Alexander Ventner does in his book, *Doing Healing*:

'The tension and mystery of the kingdom is critical to a proper theology and praxis of healing. We cannot dictate or control healing yet we cannot accept or surrender to sickness. We pray with confident authority and expectation of healing for everyone, yet we are humble and honest, trusting God with the results as only God can heal. We do both at the same time. We instinctively try to resolve tension by tending to "either/or" because "and/both" is messy). Too much "kingdom now" leads to arrogance and presumption, demanding healing as if on tap. Too much "kingdom then" leads to pessimism and fatalism, leaving healing to "if it is God's will". Balance leads to a neutralising of the radical edges, loss of risk-taking, a passive middle road and theologically correct approach to healing. We too easily explain lack of healing by kingdom tension when we ought to push through in faith. Embracing both the "already" and "not yet" of the kingdom, makes us living paradoxes. It is learning to live and minister in the over lapping of two ages: the power of the kingdom and the resistance of this age. It leads to persevering faith, optimistic realism, dependence on God, discerning the moment, honouring people's dignity, respecting the unknown, and leaving the results with God.'[4]

You could put that on your fridge and read it every day and never get bored! We navigate the tension of the now and not yet of God's Kingdom, through embracing it all. This means I can embrace the mystery of why we don't always see immediate breakthroughs and stay joyful, and at the same time never give in to sickness, impossibility or pain. We prophesy from this glorious perspective!

Core Kingdom Values

I was greatly provoked listening to Kris Vallotton,[5] who suggests that we need to live from core values, in order that our stances define our circumstances, not the other way around. One of the ways we can create a healthy prophetic environment rooted in a Kingdom worldview is to define how we are going to live and what we are going to live from. Inspired by this, I have written eight core values to define how I want to operate as a prophetic minister.

1. Victory: I will not embrace a worldview that re-empowers a disempowered devil, for Jesus has already won the victory. I live on the offensive, not the defensive, because I carry the Kingdom of a victorious Saviour. My prophetic calling will inspire the generations and nations to live victoriously, even through suffering.

2. Hope: I will embrace a worldview of hope that confidently expects good things to happen, for Jesus' Kingdom always brings promise, favour and destiny to those on whom it comes. I believe the last days are days of promise, not judgement – I will be a prophet who purveys hope and faith and not condemnation.

3. Legacy: I will embrace a worldview of heritage and legacy and will not tolerate any mindset that undermines my believing for a positive future for my children's children's children, for Jesus has empowered me to perpetuate His legacy in my family and in the Church. I will live to be a prophetic father who empowers others long after I am gone and multiplies ministry whenever I go.

4. Restoration: I will embrace a worldview of restoration for ruined cities, cultures and environments, because Jesus' Kingdom will have dominion over all the earth. I will not limit my perspective to individual lives only, but to the fate of the planet itself for God has called me to make disciples of all nations. I will seek to be a prophetic voice not only of restoration in the Church but reformation in the nations.

5. Goodness: I will not embrace a worldview or eschatology that undermines the absolute nature of the goodness of God, for Jesus has demonstrated what true love and goodness really looks like. My prophetic ministry will magnify God's goodness because the cross and empty tomb are God's final word on the nature of His character and the intentions of His heart towards us.

6. Celebration: I will embrace a worldview of celebration and thankfulness and refuse to allow the pessimistic spirit of the age to steer my heart or joy, for Jesus has already secured both. I will feed myself on good news, because what I behold I will become. I will be a prophetic mouthpiece of righteousness, peace and joy, for this is what the King's Kingdom looks like.

7. Responsibility: I will take responsibility for my generation and believe God for His promises in my day, for Jesus has ushered the future into the present. I will not push the promises of God into a time zone that can't be obtained in my generation and therefore take away any responsibility I have to believe God for them in my lifetime. I will be a prophet who takes responsibility for building wisely, expecting much and loving well.

8. Mystery: I will allow room for mystery in my life, because the Kingdom has not yet fully come. I realise that what I don't know can undermine what I do know, so I will choose to focus on the things revealed rather than the things concealed, because I know that God works out all things for my good. I will allow mystery to lead me to worship and not withdrawal, for God is my ever present help. I will be a prophet who helps others who suffer, lifts the broken and offers grace to the fallen.

The good news is that God's Kingdom is better and bigger and more imminent than you and I ever thought. You and I get to participate in God's victory – we are ambassadors of this gospel of the Kingdom. You carry life as a prophetic minister of Christ. You live in the presence of the future – His world has invaded yours. Now, go and extend the Kingdom!

Notes:
This chapter was written with special thanks to the teaching of Derek Morphew, Simon Holley and Kris Vallotton.

1. George Eldon Ladd, 1996, *The Presence of the Future: The Eschatology of Biblical Realism*, Eerdmans Publishing, p262.

2. Peter O'Brien, 1999, *The Letter to the Ephesians*, Eerdmans/Apollos, p297.

3. George MacLeod, 1956, *Only One Way Left*, The Iona Community, p38.

4. Alexander Ventner, 2009, *Doing Healing*, Vineyard International Publishing.

5. Kris Vallotton, 'My Eschatological Core Values', http://krisvallotton.com/my-8-eschatological-core-values/

Chapter Two:
The Ultimate Goal of the Cross
The Restoration of Sonship

The reality is, happiness is an inside job. Culture has as much to do with the environment of my own heart and mind as it does with external circumstances. Who I believe I am, dictates how I behave. So often it is the inner dysfunctions of our belief systems that sabotage any prophetic influence we might have on the world around us. Without tackling the inner prophetic culture of the heart, it is impossible to build healthy external prophetic cultures in the Church.

I remember many years ago when I was still young in my prophetic calling, being invited into a team meeting to prophesy. I walked in already feeling my own inadequacies and aware of my need to impress those in the room in order to feel better about myself. As I looked at the impressive-looking people around me my fears got the better of me. When it came time for me to prophesy, I went far beyond the brief God had given me and deliberately added in some details of which I already had prior knowledge. The stunned looks in the room as people thought that I had nailed it, only served to feed my pride and insecurity, but inside I felt ashamed. I knew that on that occasion my fear had trumped my sonship.

Insecurity, competition, rejection and timidity have all plagued the prophetic ministry for centuries and on many occasions I have been affected by all of these and more. In many of our churches we have inadvertently created a culture of performance, which only recognises the value of prophetic people when they are 'performing' well; this has reinforced the false inner belief that my value and identity are wrapped up in what I do, rather than who I am in Christ. Instead of a culture of empowerment, we have created cultures of entrapment that reinforce the lies prophetic people already believe about themselves.

Which is why, when it comes to creating a healthy prophetic culture, building in a rock-solid understanding of our adoption in Christ is of such fundamental importance. For the apostle Paul, the building block of new creation reality was one of the key foundation stones to be laid into the heart of the churches he served. He understood that all that we do must now flow out of who we are and whose we are. Those who believe they are still slaves carry on acting like slaves. Sons, however, are free to grow up and become like their Father. Paul puts it this way:

'For those who are led by the Spirit of God are the children of God. The Spirit you received does not make you slaves, so that you live in fear again; rather, the Spirit you received brought about your adoption to sonship. And by him we cry, "Abba, Father." The Spirit himself testifies with our spirit that we are God's children.' (Romans 8:14-16)

The Ultimate Goal of the Cross
It's vital that we recover the understanding that behind God's desire and need to deal with sin at the cross, there was another ultimate and higher purpose at work in the heart of the Father. The ultimate goal and purpose of the cross was not just the forgiveness of sins, but the adoption of sons.

Behind the legality of justification was the joy of adoption! The motive throbbing in the heartbeat of God as He sent His only son into the world, was love (John 3:16). Christ's death on the cross was necessary so that sin would no longer be a barrier to us coming to know God as Father and being enveloped in the eternal love of the Godhead. The cross makes the ultimate goal of God possible: to have you in His family forever, with the barrier of sin finally removed. It is for this reason, that J. I. Packer presents adoption as the highest blessing of the gospel:

'What is a Christian? The richest answer I know is that a Christian is one who has God as his Father. If you want to know how well a person understands Christianity, find out how much he makes of the thought of being God's child, and having God as his Father. If this is not the thought that prompts and controls his worship and prayers and his whole outlook on life, it means that he does not understand Christianity very well at all . . . Adoption is the highest blessing of the Gospel.'[6]

Knowing the Father through the Son is the goal of the ages. Jesus describes this as 'eternal life' (John 17:3). Knowing God intimately is not the route to something greater, but is itself the greater thing. You were made to know Him and understand who you therefore are. You are His child.

Understanding this profound yet simple truth enables prophetic people to operate effectively and fruitfully around others, because our behaviour always demonstrates the nature of our internal world. So much of the process of sanctification is about my head catching up with what has already happened in my heart, that moment when I was first plunged into Christ and His righteousness.

I am not just a slightly better behaved version of my former self. I am a new creation in Christ, the old has gone, the new has come. I have received a complete transformation of identity. I'm not just off the hook with God, but I am one of the family, grafted into the eternal blessings of my Father's house. Now, that is something worth getting excited about!

Prophetic cultures are full of revelation about the grace of God, where sons and daughters walk free in their new identity. Here is the testimony of one man who attended a conference at our church, having received some personal prophetic ministry from our teams:

> 'For the first time in my life I was able to believe that even in some very small way God actually honoured me! Not for what I might have done or might do but as His child. (I'm 67 and have been involved in evangelism, in foreign missions and in church leadership roles since I was 20.) I realise now that a person can be so utterly convinced of their worthlessness due to being despised, ridiculed and rejected by their earthly father, that they are cut off from experiencing the Father's love. It was on Sunday morning, as I read through the notes I received from my personal prophecy session, that the dam suffered a major fracture and God's love began to flow into my heart.'

A culture of sonship enables revelation like this to flow, bringing freedom to prisoners and release for captives. It is time for the Church to herald the miracle and power of our adoption into the Father's family for all to hear. This news is too good to keep to ourselves.

The Three 'A's of Adoption

The following three truths about our adoption in Christ are crucial in creating a prophetic culture rooted in the revelation of sonship; they dismantle the deception of rejection, one of the most powerful identity lies to plague prophetic people.

a. I Am Accepted in Christ

> 'Accept one another, then, just as Christ accepted you, in order to bring praise to God.' (Romans 15:7)

Romans 15:7 tells us that this truth greatly affects the way we behave towards others. No longer am I rejected, fighting for approval. I am accepted. The cycle of rejection has been broken.

Rejection operates in an all too familiar cycle; it goes something like this: when I feel rejected, it hurts, so before anyone else can reject me, I reject them, in order to defend myself from further pain. As John Maxwell put it, 'hurting people hurt others and are easily hurt by them.'[7]

Unless the truth of your acceptance in Christ is powerfully communicated in your family and culture, prophetic ministry will veer towards two equally dangerous ditches in the road.

The first dangerous ditch of an unbroken rejection-cycle in our lives, is the development of very shallow relationships with others. I live on the surface because of the fear that if people really knew the real me, they wouldn't like what they find and I would be rejected yet again.

This only serves to create a self-imposed isolation for prophetic people which becomes an open invitation for deception. Isolated people get deceived; it is that simple. I was not made to do life on my own but in community. When we cease to have people who know the real us and speak the truth in love, we create silos of solitude where the only opinion we hear is our own. We were made to live in family, with our masks down, in authentic and connected friendships of covenant love and loyalty. If you don't have someone whose opinion you trust more than your own – because you know they love and are for you – you are in a dangerous place. Prophetic voices in our community must be deeply connected into the body of Christ, sharing life vibrantly with other brothers and sisters.

I remember very early into being on the leadership team at the King's Arms, one of my fellow leaders asked if I and another friend would spend time praying through some quite deep issues with him. He shared very vulnerably with us as we prayed together and he experienced some significant freedom. Later he told me that he had deliberately asked me to join him that day because he wanted me to know him at a much deeper level. He wanted to build trust, and trust is always the capital of great friendships. Unless we drop our masks and live authentic lives we will never shake the enemy's shame-tactics which keep us locked in fear.

In our church, we encourage everyone to have at least one or two people who know everything about us, warts and all. Our preaching team will deliberately model raw authenticity from the platform, because we want to create the expectation that this is a culture in which it is safe to be you and to be known. When prophetic people understand their acceptance, it enables courageous relationships.

Secondly, the cycle of rejection can trap us into the ditch of a risk-averse lifestyle of cautious fear. Many of us fear being rejected when we fail or our performance does not match up to expectations. Many children in the West grow up only ever experiencing praise when they get the grade A, win the school race or win first prize at school. Our whole education system in the Western world is defaulted to reward high achievers, reinforcing the belief that failure equals rejection. Unless this is exposed and rooted out through acceptance, the prophetic in your church will remain shallow, vague, safe and therefore entirely unbiblical!

A few years ago I came to a juncture in my life where I realised I had become incredibly cautious. This was brought home to me one day when my wife began discussing a long fast she wanted to embark on. When she asked my opinion, my first response was 'let's be careful, that sounds a bit dangerous!'

Gently and humbly, Carole reflected back to me, 'Phil, you have become so cautious. You never used to be like that. When we first got married you were so bold and fearless.' She then related several incidents in the recent past, where 'let's be careful' had become my stock answer. Now, sometimes 'let's be careful' is a wise response. But in my case, I knew instantly that she had exposed something that was not founded in heaven's wisdom but my own cautious fears. It set me trying to figure out where this risk-averse mindset had taken root.

A number of months later we attended a King's Arms conference in Bedford, where we would later move and join the team. At the end of one session we stood in response to a ministry time. Instantly, I felt the power and weight of the Holy Spirit rest on me. A good friend of ours who was leading the prayer time began, quite out of the blue, to command all spirits of religious control to leave in the name of Jesus. To my utter surprise I began to experience massive deliverance and literally felt something leave me and disperse into the atmosphere! It ranks among the most remarkable experiences of my life. This was quickly followed by another friend praying for a spirit of rejection to leave me, at which point the same things happened again, as I felt a heavy weight drop off my spirit.

I can honestly say, after that encounter, I was a different man. God had delivered me from a deep and wearying sense of rejection and control that had trapped me in caution for a number of years.

If the prophetic in your environment has become entirely predictable, under-whelming and lacking in anything revelatory, perhaps this is your issue. Deal with the roots of rejection and the prophetic will thrive.

Knowing my acceptance in Christ tethers me to the realisation that God, in His utter sovereignty, majesty and self-dependence, saved me not because He needed me, but because He wanted me. You and I were on His wanted list a long time ago:

'In love he predestined us for adoption to sonship through Jesus Christ, in accordance with his pleasure and will – to the praise of his glorious grace, which he has freely given us in the One he loves.' (Ephesians 1:4-6)

I remember as a fourteen-year-old praying about our family's imminent adoption of another child. We were yet to meet any children, but as I prayed I clearly felt God drop the name 'Adam' in my head. A number of months later we met Adam, my brother, for the first time, standing on the driveway of his house waiting to meet us. He was on the wanted list, chosen by name to be adopted into our family. The same is true of you.

A second aspect of our adoption which breaks rejection, is the realisation that we are affirmed by God

b. Affirmed by God

'And I pray that you, being rooted and established in love, may have power, together with all the Lord's holy people, to grasp how wide and long and high and deep is the love of Christ, and to know this love that surpasses knowledge – that you may be filled to the measure of all the fullness of God.' (Ephesians 3:17-19)

God says 'yes' to us with a love that surpasses knowledge! This means that He not only loves you but He likes you. You are called God's beloved, His prize, His treasure, the apple of His eye.

When it comes to creating security and fruitfulness in the prophetic ministry of the Church, this truth breaks the lie that affirmation only comes through perfect performance. Many of us inadvertently live for affirmation rather than from affirmation, and there is a big difference.

Performance-related affirmation causes the prophetic to fear man rather than fear God, and this traps us in a cycle of comparison and measuring ourselves against others. If the fear of God is the beginning of wisdom, then the fear of man is the pathway to all manner of foolishness. If your success threatens my opportunity to be affirmed by other people I deem to be significant, you have just become my enemy. This kind of 'prophetic jousting' creates a toxic atmosphere of mistrust and is a breeding ground for the enemy's manipulations. Competition is the enemy of community.

Mike Bickle famously recalls 'Duelling Prophets Sunday'[8] back in his home church in Kansas City. The congregation sat in shock as two leading prophetic men took it in turns to out-do one another's prophetic words. As the public competition raged each promised bigger and better things from God. This is what happens when we fail to root our behaviour in the affirmation of God which breathes His fatherly affection deep into our souls, irrespective of our performance. If I measure my worth in comparison to how someone else is doing I have traded the security of my sonship. There is a better way to live and to think.

One morning, years ago, when we first had moved to Bedford, our son Sam was struggling with school and adjusting to his new life in a new town. Suddenly it all got the better of him and he had a full-blown panic attack. Any of you who have watched someone else have a panic attack will know how alarming this experience can be.

His sobbing was uncontrollable as he battled with fear. Carole and I tried every parental trick in the book, including bribery and corruption, but to no avail. No matter what we tried, the panic continued and the tears flowed freely. Amidst the sobs, Sam began to say, 'I'm worried about disappointing you because I can't stop crying … I don't want to let you down.'

At that moment, the penny dropped and I knew what he needed. I stood him to his feet, held his shoulders, looked him in the eyes and began to pour encouragement into his ears. 'I am so proud of you, son. I am proud of you whether you cry or whether you stop. You are such an amazing boy. You are so courageous and so special to us. Nothing could make us love you more. We love you all the time, whether you are doing well or whether you are struggling. We will always be proud of you because you are our son!'

His panic instantly subsided as the powerful peace of the Holy Spirit descended into the room. Sam stood still, knowing he was affirmed by his dad, just as he was. Later that same evening, I was out at a prayer meeting and I sent him a quick text saying: 'Love you, son. Remember to pray. Jesus is with you and I am so proud of you.' He texted back simply, 'Thanks, love you.' The power of affirmation releases thanksgiving and love in those who know they are loved by the Father, just as they are.

Quite simply, if you want to live from affirmation, you need not only to receive this from God, but give it to one another. We desperately need affirmation as human beings and to have someone say to us, 'You are amazing, you are so brilliant, I love having you around, I am so proud of you.'

In our church we teach people to give and receive encouragement well. If someone encourages you, you are not allowed to bat it away and dismiss it. In fact we teach people to ask – is there anything else you want to encourage me about?!

We all need to know the Father's affirmation.

How is it with you?

c. I Have Access to God

'For through him we both have access to the Father by one Spirit.' (Ephesians 2:18)

The last death blow to a rejection mindset is the knowledge that as sons and daughters we now have full access to the Father, which breaks the old lie that I am excluded, powerless and always bound to be forgotten and left out.

One of the things I love about visiting my parents' house, even though I moved out long ago, is that I still have fridge rights because I am a son in my father's house. I feel freedom to rummage around and look for the best culinary fare, because I know who I am. I have access because of sonship in a way others would not.

Unless this message of inclusion takes root, prophetic people in our communities can detour into one of two errors. First, it can cause them to push for power and position, believing that profile equals significance. Or, secondly, it can cause a withdrawal into self-pity and apathy. I've witnessed many a prophet holding their very own pity party, where the only people invited to attend have to be more miserable than they are. There are no balloons allowed at a pity party!

Both of these reactions are symptoms of an inner belief that I am insignificant and excluded, both of which have been smashed at the cross and empty tomb.

The truth is that in Christ we have now received an 'access all areas' pass to explore our Father's heavenly resources and partake of the unsearchable riches of Christ. You don't need to influence others to have significance and authority. You are already highly significant and have been given authority in Christ. You have all you need in Him.

George Müller, the great 19th-century Christian philanthropist and pioneer, was known particularly for his believing prayer. One story serves as an astonishing example of our access to the Father at all times. It took place on a sea journey made by Müller, en route to Canada. The incident was related by a Mr Inglis, who heard the story from the captain of the ship bearing Müller.

'While sailing off the coast of Newfoundland in extremely heavy fog, George came to him and said, "Captain, I need to tell you that I must be in Quebec on Saturday afternoon." The captain told him that it was simply not possible, due to the weather conditions. George said, "Very well, if your ship cannot take me, God will find some other way, for I have never missed an engagement in fifty-seven years. Let's go down to the chartroom to pray."

'Again, the captain protested, saying, "Mr. Müller, do you realise how dense the fog is?" "No," replied George, "my eye is not on the dense fog but on the living God, who controls every circumstance of my life." The captain then told how George knelt down and prayed one of the simplest prayers he'd ever heard. When he finished, the captain himself started to pray. But to his surprise, George put his hand on the captain's shoulder and told him not to pray. "First," he said, "you do not believe God will answer, and second, I believe He has. Consequently, there is no need whatsoever for you to pray about it. Captain, I have known my Lord for fifty-seven years, and there has never been even a single day that I have failed to get an audience with the King. Get up, Captain, and open the door, and you will see that the fog is gone." The captain got up, opened the door, and sure enough, the fog was gone. And George Müller made his appointment for Saturday afternoon in Quebec.'[9]

George Müller kept a motto on his desk that brought comfort, strength and confidence to uplift his heart. It simply read, 'It matters to Him about you.'

What a truth to transform, not just prophetic ministry, but all of life! I have access to the Father, whose face is always turned towards me in passionate love and kindness, throughout all the days of my life.

Imagine the revolution that could begin with people who knew that they had access to the Father, whatever the odds, and that it is God who controls every circumstance of their lives. Everyday I have access to an audience with the King of Kings and it matters to Him about me!

A New Day

It is time for prophetic people to stop thinking like orphans, grasping for power or hiding in the shadows of introspection and self-absorption. You have been given the full rights of sons. You have access by a new and living way, opened eternally by the shed blood of Jesus. You can approach the throne of grace with boldness and confidence, knowing He receives you as precious and beloved sons and daughters.

The answer to a successful prophetic church is not necessarily better strategy, though this can help, but a real encounter with the author of love. A church that is intoxicated with the deep affections of God, will be one that cannot help but change society around them and release God's prophetic purposes into every corner of the globe. Love has always been the most persuasive motivator in the universe, because at the heart of that universe is a God who is love itself.

When we build cultures of sonship, strong prophetic people grow up in an environment where they are free to make mistakes, learn from their failures, grow in their gifting, stay humble, serve well, connect to community and honour leadership.

How do we live this way? Meditate on these truths. Declare these truths. Remember these truths. Live these truths. Make space in your life for encounter with the Father. Make space in your life for a different way of thinking about yourself. Make space in your community for His love to set the temperature. His love for you is great!

'How great is the love the Father has lavished on us, that we should be called children of God! And that is what we are!' (1 John 3:1)

Notes:

(For the audio of this message go to http://www.kch.org.uk/resources/ talks/message/adoption.html)

6. J.I. Packer, 2005, *Knowing God*, Hodder and Stoughton, pp186-188.

7. John C. Maxwell, 2004, *Winning With People*, Nelson Publishing; p25.

8. Mike Bickle, 1995, *Growing in the Prophetic*, Kingsway, p160.

9. Herald of Gospel Liberty, Volume 102, Issues 27-52.

Chapter Three:
The Opportunity of Community
Creating Prophetic Teams

I have lost count of the number of times that men like John the Baptist and Ezekiel have been held up as a model for what prophetic ministry looks like today – as if being a voice in the wilderness is a virtue to be perpetuated and isolated odd-ness to be aspired to. Despite popular belief, not all prophetic people are strange, eccentric individuals with poor social skills, an inability to form friendships and a penchant for dressing in camel-hair dressing gowns. I have met just as many eccentric pastors, evangelists and teachers in my time. People are people! They come in all shapes and sizes.

One of the most damaging stereotypes that God is breaking in our day is the idea that prophetic people fit best outside of team and family. Everything is done better in team, even prophecy. To me, this is a fundamental core value for creating healthy prophetic culture. For too long, isolation and loneliness have been the terrible twins, masquerading as normality for prophetic men and women.

Recently we took a straw poll among some of the people in our prophetic community asking what they appreciated most about gathering together. The answer that came back most frequently was, 'We just love being with people who are like-minded, who actually understand us. It's such a relief!'

Without realising it many of our churches are filled with highly prophetic people who sit in silence and isolation because they have believed the lie that they are strange, abnormal and, therefore, automatically on the edge of true community. Only when they are introduced into family with other prophetically gifted people does this lie begin to lift and the gift can begin to flow.

Community Unleashes Opportunity

One day, a well-respected leader in our community came to see me. Sitting down, she began to tell me that the things she was about to share, she had never opened up about with anyone before for fear that she would be labelled weird, eccentric and odd. She began to share incredible experiences and encounters with God that had taken place over years, from angelic encounters, transportations in the spirit and vivid Technicolor visions. On one occasion she had been transported in a vision to an African tribe, where she began to interact with children in a village. It was as real to her as the chair she was now sitting on. Only years later, when she went to care for orphans in Zambia, did she realise she was now standing in the very place she had seen all those years before.

In the past few weeks alone, she had begun to see it physically raining in one of our church office corridors and had been visited by an angel, who appeared at the foot of her bed. 'What do I do with this stuff?' she asked. We talked for a while and I tried to give some guidance, one piece of which was to ask God why he had sent an angel and what his name was. Angels in Scripture often have a name and a specific mission and are sent to serve the saints for a certain purpose.

A few weeks later, she returned and reported that the angel had shown up several times more, but only when she was in a specific and very tricky pastoral meeting with a particular individual. When asking God what the angel's name and mission was, God had told her that the angel's name was Greg (which on the face of things is not quite as impressive a name as Gabriel). However, the name Greg, she went on to say, means 'watchful'. God had sent angelic help as a sign that He was watching over her and this particular issue she was dealing with. Wow! What an incredible gift!

Prophetically gifted people like this are sitting silently in our churches, week after week, because they believe that they are alone and have no-one who understands them. The power of finding someone who 'gets us' is not to be underestimated! The creation of community always unleashes opportunity. We have to recover the value and practice of prophetic plurality if we are to see the power of the prophetic gift unleashed in the world.

Old Testament Roots

The starting point for unpicking this issue is to dismiss the myth that God always intended prophets to operate as lone-rangers. The truth is, God's plan has always been for prophetic partnership and plurality, even in the narrative of the Old Covenant.

I remember once having the opportunity to present a paper on prophetic teams with a group of elders in the UK. A week later I received a theological critique of my paper from a well-respected theologian who had been at the day, and whose opinions I really valued. One of his fundamental disagreements with what I had shared was that in the Old Testament, the primary model for prophetic ministry was the lone voice crying out against the establishment. Isaiah, Ezekiel, Jeremiah all seemingly operated on their own. In fact, at times, men like these openly criticised the established 'prophetic groups' that had become part of the institution of wicked kings in Israel.

While I agree that this is the case, and that this may well be part of the documentary of the Old Testament, his paper missed the fact that this was never God's ideal. Prophets in the Old Testament became isolated voices because of wicked leadership, not divine design. Family is always God's favoured means of grace, because family reflects who God really is.

The Heartbeat of Prophetic Plurality

We discover, for example, the early heartbeat for prophetic plurality in the response of Moses to Eldad and Medad, prophesying in the Israelite camp. When it is reported to Moses that this dynamic prophetic-duo were continuing to prophesy after the seventy had dispersed from the tent of meeting, he celebrates! Far from being outraged or moody, Moses encourages this behaviour exclaiming, 'Would that all the Lord's people were prophets' (Numbers 11:29). God's heart for multiplied prophetic voices is immediately cemented in place, later to be reflected again by the prophet Joel: 'I will pour out my Spirit on all people. Your sons and daughters shall prophesy, your old men will dream dreams, your young men will see visions' (Joel 2:28).

But it is under the leadership of the prophet Samuel that this heartbeat for plurality really begins to have lift-off. The commentary at the start of Samuel's life states that visions were rare and that for hundreds of years no-one had really heard the voice of God through the prophets (1 Samuel 3:1). Yet by Samuel's death, prophetic life is proliferating so powerfully in Israel that whole teams of prophets are in existence. Samuel had, somehow, effectively mobilised multiple prophetic voices in the nation. These prophets found themselves in community under Samuel's anointed leadership. The first reference we find to this multiplication is immediately after Samuel has anointed Saul to be the first king of Israel. Samuel says to Saul:

'After that you will go to Gibeah of God, where there is a Philistine outpost. As you approach the town, you will meet a procession of prophets coming down from the high place with lyres, tambourines, flutes and harps being played before them, and they will be prophesying.' (1 Samuel 10:5)

Sure enough, Saul encounters these men:

'When they arrived at Gibeah, a procession of prophets met him; the Spirit of God came upon him in power, and he joined in their prophesying. When all those who had formerly known him saw him prophesying with the prophets, they asked each other, "What is this that has happened to the son of Kish? Is Saul also among the prophets?"' (1 Samuel 10:10-11)

What is clear through this encounter is that prophets were operating in community and 'the prophets' were known among the people as an established group with their own identity. When Saul encounters them he comes under the same anointing they carry, and he begins to prophesy with them. This should be how a healthy prophetic team affects others. Far from creating an exclusivity that shuts others out from hearing God, effective prophetic teams equip all of God's people to hear God like they do.

The same happens to Saul's men after he has been made King, and while he is trying to kill the young David. We read:

'Word came to Saul: "David is in Naioth at Ramah"; so he sent men to capture him. But when they saw a group of prophets prophesying, with Samuel standing there as their leader, the Spirit of God came upon Saul's men and they also prophesied. Saul was told about it, and he sent more men, and they prophesied too. Saul sent men a third time, and they also prophesied.' (1 Samuel 19:19-21)

Once again prophetic plurality under the godly leadership of Samuel spills over infectiously, this time to Saul's soldiers. Wouldn't it be awesome to create such radical prophetic communities in our churches that the voice of God spreads infectiously to anyone who comes into contact with us?

Friend of Kings

At this point in Israel's history the prophetic is very much at the centre of national and spiritual life. Following on from Samuel, prophets such as Nathan, Gad and Ahijah all consult with kings. Additionally, David sets apart the sons of Asaph, Heman and Jeduthun for the ministry of prophesying, again accompanied by music (1 Chronicles 25:1). The Chronicler goes on to list the names of those employed in the king's service for this work, for ministry in the house of God. They were trained and skilled in their work. Far from being professional prophets in a negative sense, we find here the natural consequence of David's godly leadership – prophetic plurality right at the heart of worship, at the forefront of national identity. This was always God's intent!

Prophetic Schism!

The rise of the lone-ranger, voice-in-the-wilderness prophet only emerges as things begin to breakdown in the leadership of Israel. Post-Solomon, a series of dysfunctional and wicked kings begin to replace the true prophets of God with their own prophetic-puppets, men who will speak only what the King wants to hear. Loyal God-honouring prophets begin to face terrible persecution. Instead of being invited into the chambers of the king they begin to be hunted and hounded, ostracised from civic life. This reaches its height under King Ahab, and his queen Jezebel who begins to systematically silence any voice that opposes her rule:

> 'While Jezebel was killing off the LORD's prophets, Obadiah had taken a hundred prophets and hidden them in two caves, fifty in each, and had supplied them with food and water.'
> (1 Kings 18:4)

Notice here that Obadiah's response to this national crisis is to begin gathering the prophets together again. He feeds, nurtures and protects them. The same Spirit that inspired Obadiah to rescue the prophets is still alive and well!

The historian John Bright comments on this season of schism in the prophetic ministry:

> 'The prophets of Yahweh, who became especial targets of her (Jezebel's) wrath, were confronted with an unprecedented emergency; as had never been the case before in Israel, they faced reprisals for speaking the word of Yahweh (note how

Samuel, Nathan, Ahijah of Shiloh, etc., all denounced their respective kings without suffering any reprisal). The feeling that the prophet's person was inviolable persisted until the end of Israel's history (Jeremiah 26:16-19). This had serious consequences. Some prophets, being only human, yielded under pressure and contented themselves thereafter with only saying what the king wished to hear. Others like Micaiah Ben Imlah, refusing to compromise and believing that Yahweh has decreed the destruction of the house of Omri, found themselves alienated not only from the state but also from their fellow prophets as well. A schism within the prophetic order had begun which would never be healed.'[10]

In this historical context we begin to see two prophetic movements developing. On the one hand are the loyal prophets of Yahweh, though diminishing in numbers, under the leadership of Elijah the Tisbite. On the other, we have the growing band of professional, cultic prophets of the king's court who are guns for hire, brought in to prophesy only what the king wishes to hear. A great divide is beginning to open up. Both Elijah and Elisha continue to operate in the context of team, but this is a spark soon to be extinguished in a nation that will be swallowed up by wickedness, rebellion and exile.

It is only as godly leadership breaks down that we begin to find that prophetic ministry transmogrifies into the isolated and excluded model of Jeremiah and Ezekiel. The truth is, these men longed for a return to the days of prophetic brotherhood when revelation was made healthy through team and community. Isolation is not normal and is a symptom of spiritual sickness.

This lesson from biblical history should sound a warning siren for us today. How many churches are in great danger of institutionalising the prophetic once again by only allowing revelation that tells us what we want to hear? How many of us have pushed prophets to the margins of relational isolation, simply because they once brought something we disagreed with?

Godly leadership in the Church should actually create an empowering culture for the prophetic to thrive, even if that sometimes means hearing things we disagree with or dislike. By implication, to weigh and test the prophetic, we need something substantial enough to weigh and test.

One of my favourite evenings of the year is when we gather our senior prophetic team of around a dozen men and women, together with the eldership team. These evenings are for the express purpose of listening to what our key prophetic people are seeing and hearing from the Lord. I am part of both teams, so uniquely straddle these two-worlds and love seeing how these nights unfold. Our last gathering was a classic. The team began sharing, at first, fairly general and encouraging words. It was like the warm-up lap before the game really begins! But by the end of the evening the gloves were off and the prophets were taking some risks. Revelation was flying about which nations to invest in, sums of money to give away and allocate, specific people to send church planting and certain areas of life to be watchful of. It was great and there were a lot of words to weigh, not all of which I agreed with!

And that is how it should be. An empowering leadership culture creates the space for prophetic plurality to express itself powerfully and humbly, leaving room for mistakes in an atmosphere of accountability, love and authenticity. It should be a red flag for leaders if they are only ever hearing things they want to hear. You may just have institutionalised the prophetic. It is time to open the cage, feed the prophets and let them fly again.

New Testament Plurality
This kind of plurality has always been on God's heart and, therefore, it should be no surprise when prophetic plurality re-appears with the ushering in of a new covenant under Christ.

The era of the Spirit is characterised by an abundance of the prophetic in the context of family.

Roughly a decade after the resurrection of Jesus we find prophets working together again in team, travelling and ministering alongside each other.

We know, for example, that Antioch, one of the key apostolic churches of the New Testament, had its own prophetic community:

'During this time some prophets came down from Jerusalem to Antioch. One of them, named Agabus, stood up and through the Spirit predicted that a severe famine would spread over the entire Roman world.' (Acts 11:27-28)

Agabus may have been the deliverer of this particular revelation, but don't forget that he prophesied as part of a team based in one local church. Likewise, when Saul and Barnabas set out on their first apostolic mission, it is from the gathering of teachers and prophets at Antioch that they are sent (Acts 13:1).

Jerusalem, similarly, had the presence of mature prophetic plurality. When deciding who to send to Antioch with an important apostolic letter, the apostles and elders choose Judas and Silas, two key leaders, but also prophets, in that church family. We read the effect of their visit to Antioch: 'Judas and Silas, who themselves were prophets, said much to encourage and strengthen the brothers' (Acts 15:32).

Even Philip's daughters in Acts 21 could be considered something of a family team with regard to the prophetic, and they are joined in this instance by the prophet Agabus; and the word used for Philip's daughters is actually better translated 'prophetesses'.

Leaving aside John's rather lonely prophesying on the Island of Patmos, it is hard to find any spheres where New Testament prophets worked on their own or outside of a team within the context of the local church community. In Christ, God has restored His original intention for hearing His voice – community! This is the new normal.

What Should We Do?

We have seen so far that the biblical prophetic model for operating is team. What, then, should we do with this truth? I offer the following as suggestions based on what I have seen and experienced, and what I have been involved in building. How you choose to express the value of plurality will be dependent on your context and situation, but, however you do it, please just do it! Break that isolation cycle.

a. Create Community:

Leaders need to find some intentional way of gathering prophetic people together in the local church, although the way this is done will look different depending on the season of church life you are in.

In the early days of our church, around half-a-dozen prophetic friends would gather in a home once a month late on a Sunday evening. It was informal, built on friendship and led by one of the senior leaders in the church at the time. An evening would typically involve each one sharing openly what they were living with, praying for the church and receiving the Spirit together. Evenings would often go into the wee small hours of Monday morning as God would show up in some profound ways. It was not uncommon to witness prophetic friends stumbling out of a mid-terrace in Bedford, looking as if they had just encountered God in a significant way.

As the church grew into the multiple hundreds, we began to gather people more formally, because we no longer knew everyone personally. We would still meet once a month, but by invitation only. I would invite people on the basis that they were well connected to the church family, in right relationship with senior leadership, and that they carried the culture of the church and had a clear prophetic gifting. Evenings would include a mixture of training, activation, worship and sharing for up to thirty people at a time.

Currently, I gather a senior prophetic team of around a dozen men and women who meet five times a year for curry and prophetic conversation. It is this team that also meets with the elders twice a year, equips and trains others in the church and travels extensively among other churches across the world. As I write, three from this team are just landing back from a ministry trip to Japan where they have been an amazing encouragement and blessing. It is this group of men and women who now equip prophetic people across the Church in various ways, from informal coaching to larger scale training.

One of the key aims of these gatherings, whatever the size or season, is to enjoy and encounter God together. There is nothing quite like a room of prophetic people worshipping Jesus and receiving the Spirit. It is often out of these shared moments that God has directed and spoken to us very powerfully.

The one thing you will need for these gatherings to work successfully is a strong leader, one who is well-connected relationally and culturally to your church's senior leadership team. Everything stands or falls on leadership, and the best people for leading prophetic communities are those who carry strong prophetic intuition, with leadership wisdom.

b. Provide Opportunity:
Prophetic people need opportunities to grow and take risks, but in the safe environment of team. We have tried to do this in a number of ways through the years, with varying degrees of success. I remember one evening taking a prophetic team to prophesy at a young people's event. Before we began I challenged them all to ask God for specific names or addresses

for the ministry time at the end. After I had finished speaking I confidently gave two names and an address I felt God had given me. No-one responded, even after several pleas and pauses and cranking of the spiritual handle!

Thankfully, God celebrates obedience not outcome, so I handed the microphone on to the next lady in the team, who had never tried this before. She gave two girls' names. These girls not only responded for prayer, but just happened to be best friends at the same school and were sitting next to each other. I love it!

If you lead a group of prophetic people, you must be willing to take risks and fail trying, or you will always set the bar according to your fear of failure or need for comfort. The moment your reputation exceeds your risk taking, you have decided where your gift will level off and you have capped your potential for growing a radical prophetic culture. Additionally, those you lead have to learn how to process failure well, by seeing you model it to them!

Whether it is taking teams on the streets, running personal prophetic appointments, using art and having a slot for public prophetic ministry on a Sunday or giving space for people to train others – find opportunities for prophetic people to grow alongside one another in team. Not only is it a more effective way of growing people, it's also a lot more fun!

c. Encourage Prophetic Conversation:
Another way prophetic people can work together is on Sunday mornings. Currently, many of our prophetic guys sit near to or next to one another during our Sunday meetings. Partly this is just down to friendships, but it is also to help one another catch the flow of what God is saying in the moment.

When Paul writes to the Corinthians, he indicates that there is something about prophets working together that is vital in both weighing the prophetic, but also catching the 'order' of the

Spirit together:

> 'Let two or three prophets speak, and let the others weigh what is said. If a revelation is made to another sitting there, let the first be silent. For you can all prophesy one by one, so that all may learn and all be encouraged, and the spirits of prophets are subject to prophets. For God is not a God of confusion but of peace.' (1 Corinthians 14:29-33 NRSV)

Paul clearly states that the specific goal of the prophetic in public gatherings is that: 'all may learn and all be encouraged' (v31). In order for this to happen, prophets exercise self-control, preference for one another and mutual weighing of what God is saying. In working together like this, they are a living demonstration of God's character, which is peace-loving, not chaotic (v33). Team work makes the dream work!

This is, unfortunately, the exact opposite of many charismatic church services I have come across through the years, where there do not appear to be any protocols or principles concerning how prophetic words get shared. Have you ever been in meetings where there are so many diverse contributions from a completely open-mic, that by the time the last person has finished sharing your head is in a muddle and you need to lie down in a dark room? Maybe I'm the only one who feels this, but I doubt it. When the number of prophetic contributions leaves people confused, something is not working right and we will talk some more about this issue in chapter eight.

The goal is never quantity, but quality. By working in active prophetic partnership, this goal becomes easier to realise. If the aim is not so much that I get heard, but that Jesus gets heard, it enables me to work with others to help release words to the body of Christ that are timely, accurate and relevant for that moment. We get to a place of peace and clarity when prophetic people exercise proper self-control in what they bring, working alongside each other.

Often our prophetic teams will be chatting to one another, sharing burdens, feelings and impressions as God gives them. This sometimes leads to one or two of them approaching the microphone and sharing with the whole gathered church, or whispering helpful direction to the leader of the meeting. I love it when this kind of partnership leads to the increased accuracy and authority of God's word. Teaming like this increases boldness, security and quality.

Conclusion

Prophetic people need each other and this is the consistent theme of the Scriptures. I dream of the day when every local church takes seriously the call to gather and equip prophets among them. If we are going to raise up thousands of prophets, which we desperately need to do, we must get back to the biblical imperative to be 'fruitful and multiply'. The day of the lone-ranger is over. It is the era for team.

Notes:

10. John Bright, 2000, *A History of Israel*, Westminster John Knox Press; pp226-227.

Chapter Four:
Finding God's Architects
Recognising and Releasing Culture-Building Prophets

Architects are to buildings what prophets are to the Church. Prophets are those called to see and paint with words the blueprints on God's heart for His people. It is time for prophets to understand that God has called them, not to a hit-and-run ministry, but to a design-it-and-build-it ministry. Prophets are given to the Church by God to furnish the house with revelatory 'furniture' and make it a home of radical expectancy for hearing the voice of God. Now, that's an assignment I can get excited about.

The simple reason that many churches have been unable to create prophetic culture is their inability to recognise or understand the role and function of culture-building prophets in their own communities. To train dentists you need another dentist. To equip train drivers you need other train drivers. In the same way, prophets raise prophets and enable prophetic culture to grow. Grasping who prophets are, what they are called to do and how to empower them is vital in our goal of creating whole communities that are prophetic.

Ephesians chapter 4 gives us the fullest biblical picture of what culture-building prophets look like and what they do. In this passage the apostle Paul unveils God's plan for Kingdom culture creation in the Church – a culture designed to infiltrate the whole of society as it spreads out from the community of God.

'But to each one of us grace has been given as Christ apportioned it. This is why it says: "When he ascended on

high, he took many captives and gave gifts to his people."
(What does "he ascended" mean except that he also descended
to the lower, earthly regions? He who descended is the very
one who ascended higher than all the heavens, in order to fill
the whole universe.) So Christ himself gave the apostles, the
prophets, the evangelists, the pastors and teachers, to equip
his people for works of service, so that the body of Christ
may be built up until we all reach unity in the faith and in the
knowledge of the Son of God and become mature, attaining
to the whole measure of the fullness of Christ. Then we will
no longer be infants, tossed back and forth by the waves, and
blown here and there by every wind of teaching and by the
cunning and craftiness of people in their deceitful scheming.
Instead, speaking the truth in love, we will grow to become in
every respect the mature body of him who is the head, that is,
Christ. From him the whole body, joined and held together by
every supporting ligament, grows and builds itself up in love,
as each part does its work.' (Ephesians 4:7-16)

1. Grace Has Been Given

'To each one of us grace has been apportioned' (v7)

Paul starts by saying that Christ has given grace. Grace in this
context is not primarily the 'undeserved favour' we receive at
salvation, but the grace which 'divinely empowers' us to operate
in the anointing of God for a particular task.

The first time I ever prophesied, I felt as if I had been plugged
into a different power source, one that enabled me to do something
that two seconds before would have been a complete impossibility.
I was twelve years old and on a youth retreat. Just one day earlier I
had been prayed with to be filled with the Holy Spirit for the first
time and, the following evening, as I made the walk in the rain
up to the meeting, I suddenly felt God speaking to me. It was the
very first time and it cut through the other thoughts in my mind

like a hot knife through butter. It was alarming, exhilarating and surprising, all at the same time. In those days, I was incredibly shy and when the meeting leader gave an invitation to come and share any words we had from God, I sat on my hands and tried to ignore the inner impulse to go and share. Though my heart was thumping and my hands were sweating, I resisted the impulse to share and gave in to my fear.

A second time, my youth leader said, 'There is someone here and you have a word from God. Please come to the front and share.'

'There is no way on God's green earth that I am getting up in front of all these people,' I thought to myself. But for a third time my leader made the call to come and share, the waiting becoming more painful and excruciating by the second. As if driven by some unseen spiritual muscle never been exercised before, I found myself standing, walking to the front and bumbling out what I felt God had said to me. It was like a strange out-of-body experience.

Just relieved that the whole ordeal was over I made my way back to my seat, not realising that while I had been prophetically 'bumbling', one of my youth leaders had begun weeping openly as I had shared. He later told me how my word had been specifically for him and how God had met him that night. I was gobsmacked and more than a little elated. Something had been supernaturally transferred to me, which meant I could now hear God.

In that moment, grace was apportioned. Grace is like a seed. Every apple seed has a calling to become a tree one day. Life is contained within it. God plants grace seeds in our life to see what we will do – ignore or nurture them. It is only in the nurturing of this seed that the embryonic callings of God are fulfilled and life released as God intended.

When it comes to the prophetic, God Himself chooses the men and women called to be culture-building prophets. He gives the grace that enables that calling and gifting to become a reality and it is a completely free gift, utterly unconnected to character. This is scary but true! It is as we nurture these gifts from God that they grow to become callings, destinies and realities.

Four years after that first encounter of hearing God, He began to define His calling for me more specifically as I nurtured the seedling gift He had planted in my life. I was powerfully meeting with God in a church service when one of our leaders came to pray for me. It is still etched deeply in my memory. He prophesied saying: 'When others laugh, you will weep. When others weep, you will laugh, for you will see the deliverance of God coming around the corner. God has called you to be a prophet.'

Life Changing!

Grace, apportioned by God in this way, had nothing to do with me and everything to do with Him! I was neither wise, nor mature. A calling to be a prophet is never a reward for good behaviour or in recognition of outstanding achievement. In fact, God delights in choosing the weak and foolish things of this world, those earthen vessels that have little to attract us. This is God's way. He chooses nobodies and makes them somebodies.

This is also why history is full of prophets who had a clear calling but lousy character, because grace is not rooted in performance but identity. Paul was able to say about his apostolic call, 'By the grace of God, I am what I am!' (1 Corinthians 15:10).

But God has designed godly character and Christ-likeness to be the suitable vessel for His grace gifts to grow in. Peter carried an incredible apostolic call straight from the mouth of Jesus. He had been given the name 'Rocky' by Christ Himself (Matthew 16:18). His call was to be the rock, the stable one, the pillar, the foundation, Mr Dependable. Yet just a few pages on in the story, 'Rocky' starts rebuking Jesus and cutting off ears with his sword!

Peter had grace but not much substance yet. It was only as Peter's character development and calling grew in tandem, that the influence Jesus intended him to carry began to work out.

The seeds of God's grace are not planted through our efforts, but they are designed to grow healthy and strong through our participation. Only calling and character can bring about the fullness of all God designs for His gifts of grace. For this reason we must respond in two ways to this truth about grace.

First, we must keep working on the character development of emerging prophets and not believe the lie that just because someone carries huge gifting they don't need help to shape up. Culture-building prophets have to go through an intentional process of discipleship and maturity or else their words carry little resemblance to the life they actually live. Maturity happens not through legalistic behaviour modification but identity centred change. I am becoming more of who I already am in Christ – a fully accepted, included, forgiven, heir, saint and child of God! Before I can have a message, I must become a message.

I am so grateful for men who called me into a life of character development. Back in 1998 I had just finished my university studies and, with no counsel at all, had decided that I would leave the church I was in and head off into the sunset and join a new church plant. I vividly remember sitting in the lounge of our pastor at the time with my wife Carole as we announced our plan. In my immature head, this was a kind of 'good-bye' meal, a last hurrah and courtesy. Ironically, at the time I felt I was being quite mature. We had just finished dessert and all was going well. But then my pastor said, 'Phil, I think you're making a mistake. You haven't sought counsel or advice from anybody. But you do still have a choice. You could go and join that church plant and get all your gifting used or you could stay for another two years and I will help work on your character.'

Boom!

At the time I was not praising God for that advice, but I have thanked God many times since for a wise man who gave me wise counsel. He saw my calling, but knew I needed character. Do not mistake gifting for maturity. Even the grandest apple tree starts life needing support and guidance.

Alongside this truth, we need to understand that anointing comes in all shapes and sizes, often in people that look and sound different to us. God apportions His grace to some strange people! I once heard Terry Virgo, say this:

'I must respect God's anointing, even if I don't like the channel. This is a very important biblical principle. I could end up out of step with the Spirit. The giving of gifts and anointing is not a reward for sound doctrine and good church order. In the Old Testament Samson was far from perfect but God anointed him and he is in the list of faith heroes in Hebrews 11. So, while we don't want to embrace foolishness, neither do we want to miss God.'[11]

It is easy to miss those whom God has called to serve us because we cannot see past the outer packaging to the gift contained inside. God hides His treasure in jars of clay. Beware dismissing the very people God has sent to help you advance. The very prophets we need to help us develop prophetic cultures may be sitting in our own churches, unrecognised, misunderstood and un-nurtured. Often character issues and personality irritants make them easy to dismiss, but if we learn how to call out the treasure in these jars of clay, we will discover people in whom God has apportioned His grace; a prophetic grace that we so desperately need.

2. Gifted People
'That is why it says ... he gave gifts to his people' (v8)

One of the evidences of God's grace is the giving of gifts to His people. These gifts come in two forms: activities and people.

First, God gives gifts of the Spirit which are activities such as healing, faith, words of knowledge, distinguishing of spirits and the ability to prophesy, to name but a few. These are Spirit-inspired activities and abilities. We know that everyone can prophesy, because this is an activity gift given by the Spirit for all believers to flow in (Acts 2:17-18; John 10:4). All of God's children should expect to hear their Father's voice, because this is the birthright and privilege of all children. This is a divinely inspired ability which we must keep fighting for in church life. We all get to hear God, whether or not we have been following Jesus for fifty years or five seconds.

My dad once heard a retired Methodist minister share his story of coming to faith. He described how he had married a Christian lady who dragged him along to church. One Sunday, while attending worship, for some unknown reason he began to weep. He says: 'I started after the first hymn and I continued weeping for the rest of the service. I couldn't wait to get out and hide my feelings but after arriving home the weeping was accompanied with spasmodic vomiting over the course of the next few hours. It was during that time my wife suggested that what was wrong was to do with my spiritual life and maybe sin, so I should go and see the minister.'

So he did. Upon seeing the minister of the church, he quickly gave his life to Christ. The next day he woke at 3am with a desire to read the Bible. He didn't know where to start so he opened it in the middle and started to read. It was Isaiah 55 and it seemed to come alive, especially verse 12: 'You will go out with joy and be led forth in peace, the mountains and hills will burst into song before you and all of the trees of the field will clap their hands.' At six o' clock he went walking with the dog but as he walked through the fields doubts began to fill his mind. So he decided he would look for some proof that God was there. He remembered the reading in Isaiah so he stood in front of a tree and prayed: 'If you are really there move that tree.' The tree didn't move! Then he heard an audible voice saying, 'Ask me for something worthwhile and I will do it.'

The voice took him completely by surprise. The next field had sheep in it so with the dog on the lead he walked on, only to find a sheep lying helpless across the path. The sheep had a broken leg – the leg was bending the wrong way at a grotesque angle. The voice came to him again. 'Ask me for something worthwhile.' So he stood over the sheep and prayed for it to be healed. Immediately the sheep's leg straightened, the animal stood up and ran off . . . with himself not far behind!

God gives the ability to hear His voice to the young and old, men and women, mature and immature alike. It is our birthright as children of the Father. Prophecy is not for the elite or select few but every Jesus follower. This, we must always fight for.

However, secondly, God does also give gifts in the form of people. These people are not gifts of the Spirit, but gifts of Christ to the Church (Ephesians 4:11; 1 Corinthians 12:27-29). Paul describes these people gifts in the next verse.

3. The Five-fold Ministry

'So Christ himself gave the apostles, prophets, evangelists, pastors and teachers' (v11)

These people gifts are the five-fold ministry gifts listed in verse 11. Christ's gifts to His people are other people – apostles, prophets, evangelists, pastors and teachers.

Note the key distinction between a prophecy and a prophet. One is something you do, while the other is someone that you are. Big difference!

We have not traditionally been very good at making this distinction, which is why in church we have viewed the prophetic narrowly as sharing something from a microphone on a Sunday morning. We have confused someone's ability (prophecy) with his or her calling (prophet); we have confused an activity with a person.

Consequently there has been a lot of activity but, at times, a terrible dearth of gifted people who can serve churches and transform cultures. It came as a rude awakening to me, a number of years ago, that I could count on one hand the number of mature prophetic prophets known to me, that I could confidently recommend to lay prophetic foundations in other churches. It was around this time God spoke clearly to me and said, 'Phil, I want you to help raise up one thousand prophets.' By God's grace, we are well on the way as we have trained and coached hundreds of men and women across the nations. We have to get on track with God's agenda, which is not just to multiply activity gifts but multiply people gifts!

One of the reasons for this dearth of mature prophets has been our identikit, cookie-cutter view of what a prophet should look like. The truth is people come in all different shapes and sizes, even prophets. I know prophets who have exceptional dreams and are exceptional at dream interpretation. I know others who never dream at all. I know prophets who can accurately prophesy over individuals and others who prefer to pray and intercede. I know prophets who operate privately and in counselling settings, yet others have a very public gift in preaching and proclamation. I know prophets who are natural extroverts and prophets who are introverts, some who are men and some who are women. Some prophets sing, some paint, some write poetry and songs, some fight for social justice, some have leadership gifts, some start businesses, some teach, others do not. The variety is endless.

Prophets do look through the same basic grid at the world – the grid of 'what is God saying about this?', yet they can also demonstrate an incredible diversity in the way they communicate and function. Daniel and Esther are both counted as prophets in the Old Testament, even though one prophesied with his words and the other with her life. Prophets do see through the same basic set of glasses but with all the variety and diversity of every other normal human being. God loves diversity in His people gifts.

I once stood weeping in a church as I heard them trot out the age-old stereotype that all prophets are like John the Baptist: hard to connect to, eccentric and, quite frankly, odd. I wept as I thought of all the prophetic people in that community, who had just been relegated to the sidelines of obscurity – misunderstood and misrepresented.

Contrary to public opinion, not all prophets are strange individuals with poor social skills, lying on their side for a year, cooking on their own faeces, owning a camel-hair coat and eating bugs and honey for breakfast. Personally, I am quite partial to marmalade on toast.

Such stereotypes are unhelpful and demeaning and need dismantling. I have met just as many odd pastors as prophets! People are people! Instead of creating platforms for prophets to launch from we build boxes to imprison them. How many prophets are sitting on the sidelines of the Church because they do not fit the charismatic stereotype we have created for them? Prophets are crying out for creative thinking that releases their gift with all its culture-shaping potential.

I have one prophetic friend who has a passion for bringing the kingdom in the marketplace of business. In her leadership consultancy role she regularly advises and coaches directors and senior managers of major companies in the UK, but she always does so with one ear on what the Spirit wants to do. On one occasion, during a coaching conversation with one of the leaders, she received a word of knowledge for him. She said, 'I feel like you have at least two inventions that you have never taken for patent. I feel like I need to encourage you to go for it.' The man was amazed, wondering how she knew what he had never told anyone. The next coaching session, this same man came back having had a vivid dream the night before. Remembering his experience with my friend, he took the dream to her and said, 'I just wondered if you would know what my dream meant?' She interpreted his dream accurately, again leaving the man stunned and giving her a great platform for sharing her faith. Later that day at lunchtime, she found herself in the staff canteen of this major UK company, interpreting dreams for other staff members.

Amazing! Prophets are gifts from God, but they come in all shapes and sizes.

Recognising a Prophet

So how do you recognise one of these people gifts from God? Here are four attributes which should help you recognise prophets when they are standing in front of you.

i. Ability: Prophets should be able to prophesy and have a track record of hearing God in a way that consistently encourages, strengthens and comforts its hearers (1 Corinthians 14:3).

ii. Calling: Prophets should have a personal call from Jesus that they can trace and remember. Amos was going about his business when he received his call:

'Then Amaziah said to Amos, "Get out, you seer! Go back to the land of Judah. Earn your bread there and do your prophesying there. Don't prophesy any more at Bethel, because this is the king's sanctuary and the temple of the kingdom." Amos answered Amaziah, "I was neither a prophet nor the son of a prophet, but I was a shepherd, and I also took care of sycamore-fig trees. But the LORD took me from tending the flock and said to me, 'Go, prophesy to my people Israel.' Now then, hear the word of the LORD."' (Amos 7:12-16)

It is the inner compulsion of God's calling that enables the prophet to endure opposition, hardship and testing; all are part of his or her formation as a mouthpiece of the Lord. I am just doing what He asked me to do! For a prophet, that is enough.

iii. Connection: Prophets love the Church and are recognised as being good news to the family of God. They are connected in right relationship to the body of Christ. Paul's whole argument in Ephesians 4 is that prophets are not outside of the church slinging stones from a distance, but are rather inside the community, building and strengthening. The early-church prophets Judas and Silas were marked by their ability to 'encourage and strengthen the believers' (Acts 15:32).

You have to be in it to win it! Beware self-professed prophets who have no love for the local church and burn through relationships like paper in a furnace. Layers of unresolved disappointment, hurt and offence have cut many of them off from the very bride they were called to prepare. These gifts of God need loving and honouring back into community because prophets are made to be passionate for the Church and rightly connected to her. If you are reading this and recognise yourself in this description, know that a God of infinite mercy is calling you to fall in love with the bride all over again.

iv. Anointing: Prophets are empowered to carry out their God-given assignment at an appointed time, recognised by others. This is called anointing. Prophets, in a similar way to New Testament elders, are recognised by other leaders and received by God's people. It was important for Jesus to grow in wisdom and stature, in favour with God and man (Luke 2:52). There was an appointed time for Jesus' ministry to serve and be received publicly, and so it is with prophets. Anointing is the timeliness and power to fulfil what God has called you to do. It comes with an internal and external recognition.

This means that it is possible for an emerging prophet to carry strong ability and calling but still lack connection and anointing. It takes time to grow into the skin God has prepared for you and the process of preparation is not incidental. Paul wrote to the Romans because he wanted to preach in Spain (Romans 15:24). What Paul may have thought as incidental, became one of the most brilliant and stunning gospel revelations ever written, in the book of Romans. Sometimes the journey is as important as the destination. If you are reading this as someone who carries a prophetic calling and you have not yet been recognised, don't give up but keep on going. Charles Spurgeon wisely, and somewhat humorously once said, 'It was with great perseverance the snail reached the ark.'[12] God is fashioning you as seems best to Him. Enjoy the process!

4. Culture Creation in Action: Equipping and Building

The next key question is what must these men and women actually do to create prophetic culture among God's people? Paul's answer is very clear, in that they 'equip the saints for the work of ministry for the building up of the body' (v12).

What do prophets do? They equip and they build. Prophets, alongside the other ministry gifts listed in Ephesians 4:11, are called to be the divine body builders of the Church!

The idea of equipping (Greek word *katartizo*) is that of furnishing a house and of making an environment complete. When you move into a new house, a structure is not enough, it also needs filling. Prophets fill and furnish the house of God in a way that creates a prophetic people. They build the body in such a way that all in the house are consistently growing in the grace the prophet himself carries, which is the grace of hearing God speak. For this reason, one of the key markers of whether you truly have a prophet in your church is your children's ministry. If your children are growing in hearing God and moving in the prophetic, it is a healthy indicator that the right foundations and culture are being laid.

We love training our children to hear God for themselves. One morning, our kids' work team were teaching about words of knowledge, which are a beautiful gift for communicating God's heart to people. Pairing the 9- and 10-year-olds together, our children's leaders tasked them to pray for one another and give words of knowledge about a specific object in that other person's bedroom, something they had never seen. Off they went with some remarkable encounters.

One young man gave a word of knowledge to his partner, that before coming to church he had set up his Star Wars Lego under his windowsill, because when he went back home he was going to play with it. Both children, who had never met, were stunned when this turned out to be completely accurate. His sense of being known and loved so intimately by God was palpable.

My own daughter, when in the playground with some school friends, was challenged to prove that God was real and still spoke today. One of her friends said, 'If God can speak to you, ask Him what I've got in my lunchbox.' I'm not sure how you would reply to that challenge, but Lauren coolly replied, 'OK, I'll go and ask Him now.' A few moments later she returned and said, 'You've got carrot and cucumber in your lunchbox.' Her friend's jaw hung open, as that was exactly the case. Lauren's courage to both listen and believe that God could speak to her, created an opportunity for the Kingdom to break in and Jesus to be shared with her friends, even through the trivial matters of our lunch content!

You see, a prophet's job is not to do all the prophesying. He is a builder and equipper. If everyone continues to come to the prophet to find out what God is saying, we have missed the point of the new covenant of grace – we have effectively turned the prophet into a soothsayer or a go-between with God.

While I believe in seeking prayer from gifted people who hear

God, it is possible to take this route as a shortcut to building our own intimacy and friendship with God, so that we can hear God for ourselves too!

Regularly, I have people ask me to pray for them when I know they want a prophetic word of direction for their lives. That desire to hear God through others is not necessarily wrong, but it is if they think I have more access to the Father than they do. That's simply not true. The New Covenant gives us free and unhindered access to the same Father by one Spirit (Ephesians 2:18) so that we can all know God, from the least to the greatest (Jeremiah 31:34). We no longer need a prophetic mediator, because we already have a permanent High Priest who has that role – Jesus!

Yes, prophets have a vital role in prophesying and modelling how to do that well, but the primary reason prophets are given is to furnish the house – to equip God's people for works of service and create a prophetic culture. That is the main job of the prophet.

Paul unpacks this truth by giving us the three key areas in which this equipping and building takes place.

a. To Build Us Together and Equip Us to Honour
'Until we all attain to the unity of the faith…' (v13)

Prophets build unanimity not uniformity. Biblical unity means oneness, with uniqueness. My family are united but we are also very different. My daughter loves reading, my son loves guitars, my wife loves to talk, and I love sport. We are one but we are not the same.

We can celebrate uniqueness because the goal was never that we all look the same, but that our hearts are connected to the same Lord, same mission and same love. Prophets are called to build bridges of unity, not tear them down.

One of the key ways prophets can do this is through the simple power of encouragement.

Prophets need to model speaking well of their leaders, even the ones who frustrate them. The reality is your leaders are probably doing their best, and Jesus loves them. You can disagree, but do so honourably. It is no accident that at the heart of the thriving Antioch church you have Barnabas, the son of encouragement. This is what we read:

'When he arrived and saw what the grace of God had done, he was glad and encouraged them all to remain true to the Lord with all their hearts.' (Acts 11:23)

My personal opinion is that Barnabas was a prophet who later transitioned to an apostolic role (Acts 14:14). The name Barnabas literally means 'son of the prophet' and the hallmark of his ministry was encouragement and building others up, one of the central themes of prophetic ministry in the New Testament (e.g. 1 Corinthians 14:3). My own conjecture is that the apostle Paul based his observations on new covenant prophecy by watching and working with Barnabas. This is what prophets do. They build togetherness and unity.

b. To Build Us to God and Equip Us to Encounter

'. . . in the knowledge of the Son of God . . .' (v13)

Prophets are meant to equip and build in such a way that we know Jesus better. What we build is not just about innovation but invitation – an invitation to a person. All revelation is for the purpose of knowing the One all life revolves around. If your revelation doesn't lead people to Him, you may be in the wrong game!

It is for this reason that prophets are so often passionate about encounters and experience, presence and power, tasting and seeing, because our brief from God is to introduce people to a person through first-hand knowledge. Prophets help build an experiential culture of joy and grace in which God can be met personally and corporately.

Every year I host a conference called the Prophetic Forum which gathers prophetic people for training, inspiration and encounter. The goal is to create a space for prophetic people to know and encounter God more, and take whatever they receive back to their own local churches. We have had many incredible moments through the years. One such came during a worship session. As we were singing this line of a song, 'Singing Hallelujah', over and over, suddenly many in the room could hear an angelic choir joining in the chorus. The sound of a myriad of angelic voices, harmonising and singing majestically filled the room. Our bass player stopped playing, yet heavenly instrumentation could still be heard joining our voices as we adored Jesus together. It was breathtaking and spine tingling. Prophets create culture in which God's goodness is so tangible that even the angels love to join in.

Prophets can, however, sometimes be guilty of always feeling they have to innovate new ideas in order for people to encounter Jesus. The truth is prophets often have to defend a well-worn and established truth or revelation so that it doesn't get missed. Just because something is shiny and new does not necessarily mean it is of the Lord. The question for every culture-building prophet is, 'Does what I'm building increase relational intimacy with Christ? Does it connect us to Him and create pathways to encounter God?'

c. To Build Us Up and Equip Us to Stature

'. . . and become mature, attaining to the whole measure of the fullness of Christ.' (13)

The third equipping and building goal for prophets is for the body of Christ to mirror to the watching world what Jesus actually looks like. Jesus is the head of the body and, as Bill Johnson says, God wants the head and the body to be in direct proportion to one another!

If your school photos as a five-year-old are anything like mine, you will have a bad basin haircut and your head will look far too big for your body. It's not a good look and I'm glad I grew out of it! At that young age, the body is not yet as mature as it will be, and so it is with the Church. A culture-building prophet's job is to prepare the body to be in right proportion to the head. Prophets help prepare the bride for the eternal bridegroom. We are in the business of getting the people of God ready, and prophets do this through their unique gifts of revelation, encouragement and vision.

One church I know was praying for God to provide a building for social action in their community, when this prophetic word was brought in a prayer meeting:

'My church was never meant to be invisible and kept behind closed doors. My church must be visible. My bride should be captivating. It grieves me that she is ignored in the community. I am so obsessed by her that I want everyone to be captivated by her. Not like a bride at an English wedding, gliding down the aisle with people smiling indulgently at her and her acknowledging them with a little nod of her head on either side. My bride should be obsessively captivating to society; it should be fascinated by the Church. This is not intended so we can be self-seeking or because we should court attention. Attention will be given to the church because God is restoring her supernatural beauty. It is God who will clothe her and make her radiant.'

A few weeks later, the leaders of the church reread this word, just prior to visiting a property on the main shopping high street of the town they were in. The property was a former wedding dress shop!

That lunchtime, they arrived at the shop front, looked up at the sign on the front which read 'JC's Bridal Boutique'! It was as if God was saying: 'If you can't read that sign. . . !'

The church went for the property and are still using it for amazing social action outreach in the local area. Jesus wants His Church to be mature, ready, dressed and on display for the world to see!

That is what prophets do. If you want to develop prophetic culture, you have to recognise, release and restore the prophetic office as God intended it to be. It is time for prophetic multiplication!

Notes:

11. I wrote down this quote from Terry Virgo during a message at a Newfrontiers prayer and fasting leaders' gathering in 2010.

12. http://www.brainyquote.com/quotes/quotes/c/charlesspu143068.html

Chapter Five:
Stewards of Revelation
Learning to Build With What You Have

When God speaks it is always for purpose. Creating a prophetic culture means first doing something with what God has already provided. Revelation requires a response and without one God will often remain silent until we do something with what He has already said. Many of our churches are crying out for more revelation, while God is equally crying out, 'Do something with what I've already told you!'

Pouring fresh water down the drain may be fun but it wastes what is designed to refresh the thirsty; yet all too often this is what happens to prophetic ministry in many local churches. In our excitement on receiving something from God we forget to ask the next question, which is, 'What should we now do with it?'

Prophetic culture is most healthy, at both the personal and corporate level, when the people of God take responsibility to deliberately capture, nurture and activate what God is saying. Heaven's revelation is always rooted in relationship, but grows into something through faithful stewardship. When we not only listen but also respond to God's words, we are like a wise man that built his house upon the rock.

It has been my practice over many years to try and record any significant prophetic word that has been brought over my life; but a number of years ago God gave me a vision of a 'prophetic wall' in my office at work. He began to speak to me about learning to live my life from the promises He had made me, not just the circumstances that surround me. I duly printed off twenty-or-so key words and stuck them to my wall at work in order to live intentionally by the words that have come from His mouth. When God gives you specific marching orders, wisdom looks like keeping in step to His beat and not the beat of the world around you.

In the middle of these words on my office wall is this scripture: 'Timothy, my son, I am giving you this command in keeping with the prophecies once made about you, so that by recalling them you may fight the battle well, holding onto faith and a good conscience.' (1 Timothy 1:18-19)

Actively creating pathways for the prophetic enables us to fight the battle well and run the race that God has marked out for each one of us. I wonder how many people are actually running somebody else's race? Maybe God cannot trust us with a fresh blueprint because we have not learned to steward what we already have. Copy-cat anointing is a poor imitation for running in the lane God has purposely designed for you, which is activated through doing something with what God has already said.

This chapter is all about how we can build with what we already have.

Record and Review His Words

This is a simple point, but one worth starting with. If you want to build by God's words, you need to find a way to capture what He has said; to be passionate about the process of presenting those revelations in a way that helps you become them. We always become what we behold, which is why the process of recording, listening and reading prophetic words is a vital, not an incidental, exercise. The act of regular 'beholding' enables the process of 'becoming', because God's words don't just provide information, but also impartation. His words impart life to become the very thing He has spoken to us about.

The simple habit of recording revelations God gives you will serve you well over your lifetime. Collecting these precious words is like creating a treasure chest of rare jewels, each with divine purpose to release destiny and hope.

Don't keep your jewels so locked away that they are never accessible. You need ready access to God's words, like a soldier to his gun or a doctor to his stethoscope. Carry these with you at all times so that you can pray, meditate and orient your worldview by what He says is true of you. Learn to fight battles by heaven's unveiling of who you are called to be. Without this, it's easy for our lives to be shaped by momentary circumstances rather than prophetic stances. God's words to us are like a compass, showing our true north, no matter how stormy the weather may be.

Between the prophetic blueprint of God and our current life circumstances is the growth zone, also known as the pain zone! The only way to get to the blueprint is through the growth and through pain! Having a clear handle on what God has said enables us to embrace growth by fighting with what God has said. This is why it is so important to articulate the key prophetic words over your life. They enable you to fight, and fighting successfully is vital because God wants us to learn to participate in the victory of Christ through the winning of battles. Fighting, with a clear handle on the prophetic, enables us to grow.

As the apostle John receives stunning (and sometimes hard to decipher) prophecies in the book of Revelation he is instructed to write down letters for seven churches, each of which are to be delivered to the 'angel' over those localities; to the angel in Ephesus, Philadelphia and so on. Even for the angelic allies assigned to us, I would suggest, there is something vital about recording what God has said. Even angels want clarity on their assignments from God as they minister to the saints!

If I were to ask you today, which prophetic words shape the way you think about your life and calling, what would you say?

Life-defining Versus Season-shaping Words

Another helpful way to understand words God has already spoken is by understanding the difference between life-defining and season-shaping words.

Here is an example from the life of the apostle Paul. From the earliest days of his conversion to follow Jesus, Paul understood something of the life-calling God had given him. In those embryonic moments of his faith, God began to speak to him about the shape of the days to come. This message was most clearly given to a disciple called Ananias. After Saul's dramatic Damascus road encounter, God called Ananias to pray that Saul might receive his sight and be filled with the Spirit, saying:

'Go! This man is my chosen instrument to proclaim my name to the Gentiles and their kings and to the people of Israel. I will show him how much he must suffer for my name.' (Acts 9:15-16)

This was Paul's life-calling. It steered his decisions, set his priorities and helped him stay on course over the long haul. Later in his life, when others were encouraging Paul not to go to Jerusalem for fear of persecution, Paul says, 'Why are you weeping and breaking my heart? I am ready not only to be bound, but also to die in Jerusalem for the name of the Lord Jesus' (Acts 21:13). Paul knew his life's calling was to stand before kings and suffer for the gospel; it gave him courage to make the right life choices. Life-defining prophecies set your long-term trajectory.

However, Paul was also aware of season-shaping prophetic words, which directed his course in particular moments in time. A classic example would be his vision, from a man from Macedonia inviting him to come and help. Paul takes this revelation as directive for him and his team, so they enter Macedonia concluding that God had 'called us to preach the gospel to them' (Acts 16:9-10).

If life-defining words direct the long-term direction of your life, season-shaping words give you the next steps in that process. Seasons tend to shift and change, but life-defining direction does not; therefore it is important to know what season you are in so that you can live life accordingly.

The truth is, Jesus expects Spirit-filled believers to understand the seasons in which they live. Speaking to the blind guide Pharisees, he scolds them saying that they understood the weather patterns in the sky, yet were clueless about the 'signs of the times' (Luke 12:56). The word used here for time is the Greek '*Kairos*', which means a divine moment of opportune favour. *Kairos* moments are windows in time which present special opportunities to encounter the favour of God. They can last seconds, months or years, but *Kairos* moments are set by God to bring about change, if we will only recognise and respond to them. They are decisive points that set the course of the future. Jesus' inference is that we should be able to discern the *Kairos* season we are in.

In Wimber's House

A number of years ago, before we lived in Bedford, we were praying that God would give us direction for the season ahead. We knew that He was stirring us for a possible move but had no clear direction. The advice we received at the time was largely about moving to large strategic cities of influence in the world, a number of which we had looked at as possibilities for starting a new church.

Then one night I had a dream. I dreamt I was in the house of John Wimber, the late founder of the Vineyard movement, a man known for signs and wonders and his passion for the Church. In the dream, I was being shown around Wimber's house and John Wimber himself took me to his back patio doors overlooking a massive man-made lake. Don't ask me how, but in the dream I knew the lake represented the healing anointing John Wimber carried. Calmly, in his Californian drawl he said, 'Phil, that's yours if you want it. Go out and play, have some fun!'

Still reeling from this invitation, John took me into his living room where a number of friends were gathered. One of them looked and pointed directly at me saying, 'Phil, there is a lot of talk about moving to strategic cities, but God wants you to know that Bedford is an incredibly strategic place. That's where he wants you to move.'

It was a *Kairos* moment. A decisive point in time! It was an invitation from God to enter into a new season. We went on to embrace the invitation and I'm writing these words from Bedford.

It will help you on a personal level and as a church, to differentiate between prophetic words which have a life-defining nature to them and therefore set your long-term course, and words which are specific to a season. I believe many churches are stuck in an old season because there are no fresh prophetic words coming through. Seasons change. So should we! The man from Macedonia is waiting!

King's Arms Church has some clear life-defining words. We will always be a church with a heart for the poor. We will always be a resource church called to equip the nations. We will always be a church called to share the message of the Father heart of God. We will always be a church called to pioneer a demonstration of the gospel in signs and wonders.

But within that long-term prophetic trajectory, we need to learn to respond to the prophetic seasons of church life, so that we can fulfil the blueprints of God for our community. Currently, God is speaking about this being a season of rest, focus and family, so that is what we are pursuing.

What are the life-defining and season-shaping words over your life and over your church? And do you know the difference?

Create Pathways for the Prophetic

Another way to build is by creating some clear pathways for prophetic revelation to flow so that God's words shape our strategy in significant ways.

Many prophetic words go in one ear and out the other, just as quickly as they came, but if they are to actually change the culture we must be intentional about how these are given and what gets done with them.

Elders and senior leadership teams are the cultural gatekeepers in the local church; therefore how prophetic words are handled by these teams is critical to any change that comes as a result of them. Unless elders do something with what is shared, decisions will tend to be made out of pragmatism rather than the prophetic leadings of the Holy Spirit.

In our church, any significant life- or season-shaping prophetic words are emailed or transcribed. Our senior prophetic people know they can email these to me. I, in turn, have a member of the church who volunteers his time to cataloguing these words as I send them to him. Once a term he produces a brilliant summary of the key themes that have come through in that period of time, with a link to all of the original words. Three times a year, the eldership team takes a day out to pray and discuss the key themes in this document, asking if we need to adjust, change or build anything differently as a result.

Additionally, we take at least one opportunity in the year to use the preaching platform on Sundays to take stock of what God is saying to our community. We call this our 'Tuning In' series, where we try to communicate and get on God's prophetic wavelength as a whole church over the course of a few weeks.

A regular standing item on our elders' agenda is to ask, what is God saying at the moment? This is one of a number of simple ways to capture what God is saying, so that it makes a tangible difference to what we do.

What are the prophetic pathways in your community? And how are you enabling decisions to be made by prophetic revelation, rather than just pragmatic reaction?

Prophetic Consultation

In Antioch we read that there were teachers and prophets gathered together and out of this context came the great apostolic work of Barnabas and Saul. Additionally, the apostle Paul understood the dynamic partnership created by pairing gifted people together, travelling as he did with prophets like Barnabas and Silas at his side. Paul knew that apostles and prophets received revelation of the mysteries of the gospel together (Acts 13:1; Acts 15:40; Ephesians 3:5).

I've already mentioned how we bring together the eldership team with some of the senior prophetic people in our church for evenings of consultation and prayer. There is something about this partnership which, when rightly aligned, releases huge blessing across the church. Two times a year we gather these groups together, to share and pray. The senior prophetic team comprises of around ten men and women who carry a mature, proven and well-established prophetic anointing, and who are in right relationship with the elders, love the church, demonstrate our culture, have an ability to equip the saints and 'see' strategically. I gather this group personally for curry and conversation throughout the year.

When we gather with the elders, the first evening is given over to purely listen to what God has been saying to the prophets. We transcribe the evening and give the floor to hearing from God. I brief the team before we gather to come ready to share succinctly (no more than one page of prophecies), strategically, and with faith. We challenge ourselves not to hold back on these evening. We ask God for numbers, specific people, places, nations and times. The goal is that we come away with key things to weigh which inform our decision-making as a team of elders.

One evening spent together recently gave some significant revelation that has affected the way we apportion our budget next year, which overseas areas we are supporting and some areas of warning to watch out for in prayer. I can't tell you how vital this is. It can be the difference between fighting blind and having something to aim at.

Our second gathering in the year is slightly different; on this occasion the elders will share where we are going as a church and which key priorities we are setting. In this context, the prophetic team gets to prophesy into the vision and mission outlined by the eldership.

However you do it in your local setting, there needs to be some space for intentional partnership between senior leaders and senior prophets. As one apostolic friend of mine says, 'I send the prophets up the flagpole to see what they can see and then it is my job to help build it.'

Revelation Needs to be Fought for in Prayer

Another important way to build with what you have is by watering the seed of revelation with prayer.

A great example of a man who prayed prophetically inspired prayers was the prophet Daniel, who was living as a captive Hebrew in a foreign land. When Daniel realised that the prophet Jeremiah had prophesied that Israel's captivity would only endure for 70 years, he interceded for it take place! Daniel was not a fatalist and neither should we be. When God decrees something is to take place, this is not permission to wait passively, but to engage powerfully. God's words should always galvanise action, inspire thought and provoke prayer.

God in His utter sovereignty and power has chosen to join Himself and partner His will with our prayers. When we take His prophetic promises seriously and begin to agree with them in prayer, a powerful transaction takes place in the spiritual realms. Prophetic prayer enables the very things God has spoken to become a reality in our lives.

When we choose to pray regularly through the things God has said, it is like watering a divine seed, which then begins to grow and take shape in the unseen soil of our hearts. Prayer gives birth to promises. God gives you prophetic promises so that, through prayer, you can partake of their blessings.

Before we had any children, but were newly married, I was walking along the high street praying about when to start a family, when God suddenly and clearly spoke to me. He said that we would have a son and that we would start trying to conceive in the May, and would fall pregnant in July. Additionally, my wife had a powerful dream encounter where she had a son and was instructed to call him Samuel, with God promising that he would bring delight to her heart. These were precious promises from God, all of which came true. However, this does not tell the whole story.

During my wife's second pregnancy she had our son four weeks early and he was quickly diagnosed with under-developed lungs. I still remember being the first to hold him in my arms as his little concave chest struggled. The diagnosis was uncertain and for two weeks he battled for life in an incubator. The only amusing thing in those weeks was seeing our son, a chubby 8lb baby, in his incubator alongside babies half that size. He looked like Goliath!

Not knowing if he would live or die we were both in bits, to the point where we feared to even give him a name. The thought that he might not make it was more than we could bear, so it seemed safer to hedge our bets and play it safe. We reasoned, in our emotions, that if he died, our dreams would die with him. It was too painful to contemplate.

In those moments, you are looking for any kind of anchor

to hold on to, in particular prophetic promises from God. We did what we knew to do. We began to fight with our promises. Everyday as I left the hospital to go back home, often through tears of agony, I would cry out to God and remind Him of what He had said to us.

'God, You said we would have a son! You said he would delight our hearts! God, let him live – we agree with Your promises!' This culminated in us eventually deciding, in faith, to name him Sam just as God had instructed, despite our fear he would not make it. Remarkably, from the very moment we named him officially, he began to recover. There was something about our prayerful alignment with God that enabled the very promises He had given to come about. Sam, now over six-foot tall and eating like a horse, still lives up to his name Goliath!

When you pray, you are partnering with God in ushering in the victory that is already His. Prayer is not overcoming God's reluctance but rather laying hold of His willingness. Jesus has won the victory, but in prayer we get to distribute the spoils of war. We always pray from the perspective of victory and prophecy is meant to draw you into the place of joyful intercessor, not passive spectator.

Revelation Can be Added to or Subtracted From!
Another important truth about revelation from God we can easily miss is that it is relationally rooted and flows from intimacy; this means God can add to or subtract from the things He has already said. Before you throw this book away and label me a heretic, I don't mean that God will ever change the revelation of Himself and His ways as recorded in Scripture. Those words must never be added to or subtracted from as THE authoritative word of God. What I mean is that prophetic revelation does and will shift, if we walk with the Lord and stay attuned to His voice in the different seasons of life. Relationships

require ongoing communication.

God's design is that we live life in red-hot connection with Him, not the lukewarm, autopilot that we can often find ourselves drifting into. Living relationship means living instructions.

Imagine how different Abraham's story would have been if he had failed to listen to God's second set of instructions on the mountain! Having obeyed God's first set of instructions to kill his firstborn son Isaac, Abraham is just about to plunge in the knife when God halts him, saying, 'Stop! Now I see that you fear Me!'

I'm so glad that Abraham knew God well enough to hear His voice in the moment. What I find profoundly challenging is that Abraham had neither a Bible nor an ancestry that steered his ability to know God's character and hear His voice. His knowledge was not rooted in tradition or religious history, but radical relationship. Abraham walked so closely with God that he could hear His heartbeat and knew the nuance of His voice. No wonder he was called 'the friend of God'.

Is There Anything Else You Want to Say About That?

God sometimes wants to add to what He has already said to you. Part of building with what you already have, is asking Him if He would like to say anything else about those revelations. Years ago, I spent a fruitful day walking on the beach, Bible and notebook in hand, asking God about 20 key prophetic words over my life. I spent time praying about each word in turn, writing down anything else God wanted to add or say. It was wonderful to see how God added definition to these as I prayed and sought Him. Many general words became very specific that day. One example from that day, is that God instructed me about what exact percentages of my time He wanted me to devote and spend on local, national and international ministry respectively, a revelation that has steered my decisions about how I spend my time ever since. Just because you have one word from God, does not mean that is all God wants to say about it. Ask Him!

The apostle Peter reveals something fascinating, saying, 'Concerning this salvation, the prophets, who spoke of the grace that was to come to you, searched intently and with the greatest care, trying to find out the time and circumstances to which the Spirit of Christ in them was pointing when he predicted the sufferings of the Messiah and the glories that would follow' (1 Peter 1:10-11).

In other words, the prophets of old were very deliberate and focused in their pursuit of more information. I imagine men like Isaiah, seeking God intently and therefore being told of the circumstances and nature of Jesus coming. Stunning and detailed prophecies like Isaiah 53 could well have come from Isaiah taking time out to walk on the beach and asking if God wanted to say anything else more specific. God loves seekers. He unveils His heart to those who long to know it. It is the glory of kings to search a matter out (Proverbs 25:2).

These, then, are some of the ways we can build with what God has already given us. As we take seriously the call to water the seeds of revelation, oak trees of righteousness will grow in our communities. Prophetic culture is activated as we take action.

What action do you need to take so you can build with what God has already said? A prophetic culture of increasing revelation will always, at its heart, address the core issue of stewardship, because this enables us to build something that not only lasts, but also grows from one degree of glory to another.

Do something with what you already have, and watch it grow!

Chapter Six:
Prophetic Activation
Creating the Spark That Keeps on Burning

Learning to activate prophetic gifting is profoundly important because hearing God changes lives.

One afternoon, a team from our church was hanging out in the town centre to pray for people and seeing what the Lord wanted to do. A security guard working in the town centre made a bee line for them and asked outright, 'Can you really help me and tell me what God is saying?' What an invitation!

As our team started to pray, prophetic revelation began to flow as God revealed His heart for the man. Among other things they prophesied about hope being rekindled and severed relationships restored in his life. As they prayed and prophesied, tears began to stream down his cheeks and he looked at them in astonishment. 'How do you know all these things?' he gasped. He then explained what all of their words had meant. His wife had recently left him taking his two children with her, and he was unsure if he would ever see them again. He felt bereft and hopeless, but something in their words had sparked life and hope in him again. The team explained that Jesus is alive and that He knows everything that's going on. When one of the team offered the man the opportunity to know Jesus for himself, he simply replied, 'I've been waiting to meet Jesus my whole life – yes please!' They led him to open his heart to the Lord right there and then on the streets. It was easy!

Activating the prophetic in your life, in your family and your church matters because when you learn how to hear God's voice it has this mighty potential in every situation you find yourself in. Imagine the culture-changing possibilities if believers truly grasped hold of their inheritance as God's children of hearing the Father's voice with clarity. The world could be changed.

Just as children have a natural process of language and communication development so we need to think carefully about how we nurture the innate ability every spirit-filled believer has to hear the Father's voice. Jesus expects sheep to be able to understand the shepherd (John 10:4), to the extent that they should be able to differentiate between the shepherd's voice and a stranger's.

Hearing the Shepherd is not a gift reserved for a few prophetically minded sheep. It is for all who know the Shepherd. But this God-given inheritance needs nurture and activation. A million-pound investment has been made in the bank account of our soul but it takes some deliberate steps to start drawing down what has already been deposited there.

This chapter looks at some of the ways we can nurture an environment that gets us moving in our prophetic ability, and it all starts with enabling the right mentality.

An Activation Mentality

To develop a culture of activation that allows people of all ages and stages to grow in hearing God's voice, a new mindset needs to be encouraged and reinforced – the mentality of experimentation.

At one level, to say that we 'experiment' with God's voice, sounds, well, almost blasphemous, which is why many of us avoid this when it comes to helping people grow in the prophetic. But unless we adopt a developmental approach to hearing God, we will not grow in the way God intends. Practice makes perfect.

The natural way in which we develop new skills is through trial and error. Children learn to talk by listening, assimilating ideas, copying, babbling and attempting to articulate words. In the first years of my daughter's life we were on the verge of being referred to a speech therapist; she used words that seemed to mean a lot to her but not a lot to anybody else! Then one day, as we were passing a shop-front window, she suddenly pointed from her buggy and said in perfect English, 'I really like that dolly, Mummy!' All the while, without us realising, she had been learning through a process of trial and error, and this eventually led to clear communication.

The core values of a research and development factory are different from that of a manufacturing plant. Manufacturing requires zero defects. Research and development requires them because a core value is trial and error. Great discoveries are made when we commit to the core value of experimentation in the prophetic. People have to know that it's OK to learn and have a go in an environment where they will not be scolded or punished for 'getting it wrong'. If we create a 'zero defects' mentality we will never activate the prophetic.

It is not that we should settle for mediocre, half-baked words that fail to inspire or help anybody. The goal is still 1 Corinthians 14:24-25, where people encounter God because the secrets of their hearts are revealed. It is just that the route to get there is through a whole lot of trial and error – giving things a go in an appropriate setting!

Simply put, this means we need to give people plenty of chances, plenty of gentle feedback and plenty of encouragement.

The Power of Fatherly Encouragement

When I first began to dabble my toes in the water of prophecy as a teenager, it was simple encouragement to have a go that brought the gift to life in me. As a young man, I owed a lot to a number of men who spent time with me and nurtured me in my faith; one of these was my good friend Bob.

Bob was a massive encourager and without him I don't know if I would have ever attempted to keep growing in the prophetic.

But he encouraged me so consistently to have a go that little by little I began to get better at hearing God.

Bob's regular practice was to sidle up to me in a meeting and quietly ask, 'So what do you think God is saying then?' Sometimes I would have something, at which point he would then ask me who it was for! Usually not having a clue, he would simply say, 'Well, just ask God and I'll come back in a few minutes and see how you're getting on!' Sure enough, he would return and encourage the next bit of revelation out of me. I distinctly remember one occasion as he came back, saying to him, 'I think it's for that girl over there, the one with the ginger hair.' He promptly said, 'Yes, you're right, it is. Let's go and pray for her!'

If that process were not valuable enough, the really powerful bit would happen a few days after those mini-adventures had taken place. Without fail, often on a Wednesday morning, a card would drop through the letterbox. It was from Bob and would usually say something like this: 'Phil, this is just a quick note to say how proud I am that you chose to take a risk last weekend. Well done for stepping out. I love the way you hear from God. Keep going. I am praying for you. Your friend, Bob.'

This dear friend cultivated an atmosphere in which I had permission to have a go and grow in my gift. His fatherly love, encouragement and feedback enabled me to learn and not give up, knowing that even if I made a mistake I would still be accepted.

Fatherly and motherly encouragement is crucial in developing an activation mentality; it gives us permission to experiment. If we work hard to make this the culture of our families, friendships, small groups and churches, then we have a very good chance of actually developing some healthy prophetic people who know how to hear God and give it away to others.

The Language of Activation

Of equal importance in a culture which will activate the prophetic is having a common language for the ways in which God speaks.

The panorama of Scripture provides us with a dizzying number of forms in which God communicates with His children, yet we often reduce these to a few 'acceptable' ways others may hear from God.

These days, Peter would probably be labelled 'new-age fringe' for hearing God in a trance (Acts 10:10), Ezekiel a con-artist for claiming to be lifted up by a lock of his hair and transported between heaven and earth (Ezekiel 8:3) and Daniel would be accused of drawing too much attention to angels because he mentions how the angel Gabriel directly delivered him a message from God (Daniel 9:21).

We must recover the biblical language of revelation, which includes the ordinary juxtaposed with the extraordinary. God speaks to us out of relationship, which means how you hear from God is likely to be very different to the way I hear from God. Revelation is never formulaic, it is rooted in intimacy, therefore we need to put back on the table all of the relational tools God uses to communicate with His children. If it's from Him, it's all good!

For too long, fear of excess or error has diverted our attention and in the process we have settled for shallow revelation which feels preferable to taking risks. I am not arguing that we sign up for a lobotomy and throw ourselves headlong into stupidity; but I am arguing that we need to recover the Bible's rich pallet of colours for painting God's pictures. God longs to speak through the multitude of Technicolor options He has available to Him, but many do not feel they are allowed to hear Him in these ways. We must make it a priority to educate, train and normalise revelational diversity in our church settings.

Now is not the time to take a detailed look at all the ways God speaks because many other excellent books have done this already. However, here is a selection of the weapons we need as part of our prophetic armoury. They broadly fit into the three categories of revelation – seeing, feeling and hearing. For each of these I am going to suggest a few activation exercises to help stimulate growth in these areas. They can be used individually or in groups and are simple ways of helping people grow in revelation.

1. Seeing

Pictures: God uses images, in either the natural or the mind's eye, to communicate revelation. For the young Jeremiah this was how his prophetic journey began, with God simply asking him, 'Jeremiah, what do you see?' Jeremiah replies, 'I see the branch of an almond tree.' God's assessment of that encounter was, 'You have seen well, for I am watching over my word to perform it' (Jeremiah 1:11-12 NRSV).

Often I will suddenly be aware of an image or impression in my mind's eye that wasn't there seconds before. In those moments, we simply need to ask God what He is trying to say. This can also happen physically when we feel our attention arrested by a particular object or person. When I am asking God to give me words for people I will often sense Him highlighting a particular person to me; this is His way of drawing my attention.

Dreams: Prophetic dreams are seen throughout the Bible, whether Jacob dreaming of angels going up and down a ladder at Bethel or Pharoah dreaming of seven years of plenty and seven of famine in Egypt. God will often use dreams to communicate warnings and other important information to us in order to avoid as much interference from our natural senses as possible.

I rarely dream, but my wife does, most nights. Through her prophetic dreams I know people whose lives have (literally) been saved, relationships restored and destiny revealed. Dreams are powerful!

Visions/Trances: Visions are images from God that appear super-imposed upon either the mental or actual landscapes we are viewing at the time. It is possible for visions to be so real that we only later understand that it was an open vision at all. This seems to have been the case when Peter was released from prison (Acts 12). Luke simply says 'he came to himself' (Acts 12:11).

I know people who see open visions like watching a movie on a cinema screen right in front of them revealing what God is wanting to do. I know others who see 'internal visions', as the Lord paints on the canvas of their minds.

Trances are similar to visions, but seem to be accompanied with a lack of awareness of one's surroundings at the time the experience is happening. While the New Age movement has stolen the concept of trances, the patent still belongs and originates from God, who still uses this as a means to communicate. The Greek word used in the Bible for trance is *ekstatis*. In the Greek Old Testament it is used for the deep sleep God sent on Adam in Genesis 2:12 and on Abraham in Genesis 15:12. The New Testament uses it in connection with two mighty apostolic figures: Peter in Acts 10:10 and 11:5 and Paul in Acts 22:17. W.E. Vine explains this state as 'a condition in which ordinary consciousness and the perception of natural circumstances were withheld, and the soul was susceptible only to the vision imparted by God'.

Activation Exercises for Seeing

Object Prophecy: Pair up with another person and ask God to highlight a particular object in the room and use it to speak to your partner. Spend some time allowing God to focus your attention on a particular thing and then use that object to form an encouraging prophetic word. I have used this exercise all over the world and found that it is a great way to get people using their 'seeing senses' in ways God can use. Once you have prophesied ask for some feedback. Was it encouraging and was it helpful?

Picture Prophecy: Close your eyes and ask the Holy Spirit to give you a simple image or picture in your mind's eye. Take the first image that comes along and then ask God to tell you what it means and who it is for.

Again, I have seen this simple tool help many people get started in hearing God. When my son was six he came into the bathroom and said, 'Dad, God never speaks to me!' I explained about seeing pictures and asked if he wanted to give it a go there and then. He sat himself down on the toilet and assumed 'receiving position' with his hands out and eyes closed. I asked the Lord to show him a picture and then asked what it was that he had seen. 'I can see a picture of you praying in your bedroom, but I don't know what it means,' he replied. We asked the Lord to speak again and tell Sam what it meant. Quick as a flash, Sam said, 'Dad, I know what it means. God wants you to pray more!' Not only was it a very funny moment, it was also a very accurate message from God for me. Give it a go and see what the Lord shows you.

2. Feeling
Impressions/Burdens: God speaks through growing impressions and burdens which are often the gift of discernment at work. Often these impressions grow over a period of time and become unshakeable concerns an individual carries for specific people or situations. These are then used by God to direct our prayers, our compassion and our attention as we look to respond to what He is saying.

Intuition/Perception: The prophet Daniel announces 'I, Daniel, was troubled in spirit' (Daniel 7:15) as he considers the visions he has been seeing. It leads him to ask God what they mean. This is a great way to approach strong feelings that come to you out of the blue, through which God may be trying to communicate. These perceptions can reveal enemy schemes, prayer strategy or angelic activity. Regularly, as we are driving along the road, my wife will suddenly spot someone and say, 'They looked really sad,' and begin praying for them. These are not random thoughts but Holy Spirit directed moments to get us praying in step with Him. When you feel things like that, do what Daniel did and ask, 'What is the meaning of these things?'

Bodily Reactions: God created our whole beings to be able to hear, sense and perceive Him, including our physical bodies. It should come as no surprise, then, that God speaks to us through our physical senses. I regularly feel heat in my left hand (why only my left is a mystery!) when I know God is releasing anointing for healing. Words of knowledge for healing can also often come through bodily sensations which indicate where God wants to operate in healing.

One morning, I had a sudden pain in my chest as I was preparing for a Sunday service. Attempting to shrug it off, I carried on praying, but the pain grew worse. It was only as I thought, 'Perhaps this is a word of knowledge of healing', that the pain instantly disappeared! At the end of the service that morning, I gave the word of knowledge and a lady came forward with a chest infection, but she was about to get more than she bargained for. As two of our ladies prayed with her, she met with God powerfully, resulting in complete freedom from years of terrible and dark depression. After several weeks testing her healing out and feeling lighter, she saw her own mother, who was also suffering from long-term hereditary depression. In sharing the freedom God had brought to her, her mother was instantly healed in her armchair as her daughter prayed. When she went back to her doctor for an increase in medication, she was told she had no need for it any more! All of this came from a simple bodily reaction caused by the Holy Spirit. Your heart and your flesh are designed to feel and respond to Him.

Activation Exercises for Feeling

Words of Knowledge in Your Body: Ask God to highlight which conditions He wants to heal by asking Him to highlight them on your body or emotions. Pay attention to the sensations you feel and then share them and ask for a response. Then believe God for some miracles!

Prayer Walk: Go on a prayer walk and ask the Lord to give you discernment through perceptions and feelings about the issues which need prayer in your neighbourhood or town. Pay attention to how you are feeling as you enter particular parts of your town. Stop and ask God what these mean and then pray, in Jesus' name, the release of His purposes.

3. Hearing

Actual Words: For some people, the main way they catch revelation is through actual hearing, either through the internal voice of God or His actual audible voice. This certainly happened with Saul of Tarsus on the road to Damascus as he heard the voice of Jesus in Acts 9. In verse 7 it says the other men stood by and heard a voice but they did not see anyone; but Saul heard an audible voice.

I frequently hear God internally and revelation tends to come in single words, sentences or paragraphs. For example, I was praying yesterday about a particular couple in our church, and the Lord simply said, 'You will have a long and fruitful partnership with them over many years.' It is easy to dismiss such words as mere imagination, but over the years I have learnt that these internal scripts are more often written by the

Lord than by me. Some of this stuff, you just couldn't make up. It has to be God!

I remember being newly graduated, highly educated but six-months unemployed and with a pregnant wife and bills to pay. I was out prayer-walking one day and feeling more than a little glum about the situation when the Lord super-imposed a paragraph in my mind. Clear as a bell, He said to me, 'When you get home, your employment agency will call and offer you a job, which you are to take. But it is not the final job I have for you. In two weeks' time you will have an interview for the job I have reserved for you. Get ready!' It came just like that, in one hit. Thinking I had probably made it up, I went home and waited by the phone. To cut a long story short, it happened exactly as He said it would and it was a lesson to me about paying attention to God-sentences in my head. Your imagination and thought life are not only a battleground, but more importantly a revelation ground.

Visitations from Angels: Angels are messengers sent from God to minister to the saints and frequently show up in Scripture to help, guide, warn and strengthen believers. An angel came to Daniel to bring him understanding. Angels came to Abraham. Mary spoke with the angel Gabriel, the same archangel who communicated to Daniel. Joseph was ministered to by an angel through a dream, as was Jacob. This is a far more regularly occurring experience than we realise and is still part of God's playbook when communicating with His people. We have people in our church community who see angelic activity very easily and have learnt what to do with the things they are sensing and seeing.

Often what they see enables us as leaders to direct ministry or prayer in certain ways. At a public level, we will almost never share stories of the angelic because it can easily confuse or distract. But privately, many revelations come through an awareness of angelic activity which helps direct meaningful action.

Activation Exercises for Hearing

Blindfold Prophecy: Form a group of at least six people and choose one volunteer to be blindfolded. Once the blindfold is on, the rest of the group silently re-arranges themselves so that one person is standing behind the blindfolded person. Not knowing who the individual is, the blindfolded member of the group now spends a moment listening to God and prophesying over whoever is behind them. The goal of the exercise is to help people to hear God using their spiritual senses, not some physical reading or their knowledge of an individual. This exercise also aims to help people overcome their fear of failure. Rarely will an individual get everything right, but it is a great opportunity to receive feedback and much encouragement for having a go.

Once in New Zealand, a lady volunteered for this exercise, never having heard God before. Blindfolded, she prophesied over another woman behind her. She described a picture of a beautiful pink flower, a hyacinth, floating in a bowl of water. The word was simple. God says you are beautiful like a hyacinth! Little did she know, as she prophesied the lady behind her was suddenly so impacted by the Spirit of God, that she fell onto her own sofa and began to encounter Him powerfully, the reason being, her name, Jacinta, is the Greek word for hyacinth – a 'pink flower'! That evening she also received physical healing as we prayed. It was quite a night!

Bedroom/Relatives Prophecy: Pair up with someone else that you don't know well and ask God to give you a word of knowledge about a specific object in that person's bedroom. Share and give feedback. You can also try this exercise asking God for the names of specific relatives in that individual's family that you have never met before. The goal of this exercise is to get you asking and listening specifically to the Lord, as well as helping you see that getting it wrong is part of growth and learning. The more you do this the more accurate you will become. Remember, the reason we practise in the family, is so that we get it right on mission!

One of our young men was sharing his faith with two gentlemen on the streets of Bedford when they mocked and challenged him by saying, 'If Jesus really is alive, ask Him what our names are then!' Unfazed, he asked God, told them their names and the Kingdom showed up that day! The reason we do exercises in the privacy of our church communities and families is so that when the gifts go public they have teeth, tempered and made viable by time spent in development and activation. This stuff matters. The world is waiting for an authentic revelation of God's heart through His people. How are you going to activate what the Lord has given you?

Chapter Seven:
The Rudder on Your Ship
Harnessing the Power of the Tongue

On October 30th, 1938, H.G. Wells' science-fiction novel *War of the Worlds* broadcast to Americans tuning in for a special Halloween broadcast. The first two-thirds of the presentation consisted of Orson Welles reading a series of news reports giving the impression that Martians were actually invading the planet in real time. His descriptions were so vivid and presented with such factual assurance that many listeners headed for their cellars in panic, fearing that aliens were actually on their doorstep! What was meant to be a storybook had become a news report in their imaginations. Words have incredible power to excite, ignite and put to flight!

One crucial wineskin issue for the prophetic is that of our words. If prophesying is speaking the future into being then we need to create a healthy speech and thought life which brings the right kingdom into focus around us, because words have both constructive and destructive power. This is critical to a prophetic culture.

Patterned after God
One of the reasons our words have such power is that we were patterned and designed in the image of God Himself, and His words literally create and sustain galaxies and worlds. There are at least three components to the nature of God's words and what they do.

a. Create: 'By faith we understand that the universe was formed at God's command, so that what is seen was not made out of what was visible' (Hebrews 11:3).

Living matter is physically created when God opens His mouth because He is the divine Creator. The very first revelation of God's character is as a creative being, with unlimited intelligence and panache, enabling beautiful and glorious things to come into being. God's words have in them the very DNA of life. When God speaks, invisible realities become visible galaxies. His words create the very ecosystems in which we breathe, live and survive.

b. Sustain: 'The Son is the radiance of God's glory and the exact representation of his being, sustaining all things by his powerful word' (Hebrews 1:3).

God's words also sustain all life in the ecosystems and worlds He has made. His words give ongoing support and sustenance to His creation, so that each breath we breathe is a gift from His hand.

c. Nourish: 'Man does not live on bread alone but on every word that comes from the mouth of the LORD' (Deuteronomy 8:3).

God's words also give ongoing health and nourishment to the human soul. He not only sustains what He has already made, but adds life and joy through the process of opening His mouth and speaking words of grace and love to His children. You and I are not really alive unless we are hearing the active words of God to our soul in the present tense! The reason that God fed the Israelites daily with manna from heaven in the wilderness was that we too would learn that we need the daily provision of His words from heaven. His words nourish us in our deepest parts. The 1974 beer slogan said it best, 'Heineken: refreshes the parts others beers cannot reach!' How much more is this true of God's active words which refresh us deep within, places beyond the scope of the world's reach.

Because you and I are patterned after God and made in His image, our words have the same qualities. Our words have the power to create, sustain and feed spiritual ecosystems in which we either thrive or decline. Our words are powerful which is why the prophetic is such a dynamic tool to create the right kind of life!

Prophecy Creates the Future

I recently prophesied over a church pastor that breakthrough would come in his church as he began to intentionally engage in street work with a particular young man in his church. Writing to me a few weeks later, he told of some stunning miracles that had taken place as he acted in obedience to the word God had given him. One of these included a wheelchair-bound lady that he and his friend had prayed for in a local coffee shop. This lady had no use of her right arm due to suffering two strokes and twelve mini-strokes over a number of years. After prayer, she began to move her right-hand fingers, much to everyone's delight, especially hers. A few days later, this lady called from her care home to say that she had subsequently regained total mobility in her right arm, an arm she had been unable to use for ten years! Additionally, she had also regained her long-lost sense of smell and taste. My friend commented to me in an email, 'This has been an astonishing couple of weeks – just stunned and in awe of God – wow. I am amazed at the impact of swift obedience to a prophetic key being released, and how easily it could have been missed!' What this and many other stories like it reveal, is that prophecy, when combined with our faith and cooperation, not only predicts the future but helps to create it.

The writer of the proverbs even goes as far as to say this: 'the power of life and death is in the tongue' (Proverbs 18:21).

Our words have the ability to create, sustain and nourish life or death, as well as the spiritual environments in which we grow.

Prophetic culture has to be built from an understanding that our words are creating worlds because of our image-bearing nature.

Visiting a friend in New Zealand, I remarked on the huge tree in his back yard, to which he replied, 'Yes, I planted that tree just thirty years ago!' I was stunned that such a large, mature-looking tree could grow to such a substantial size so quickly. He went on to explain how the humid Pacific climate of New Zealand offers plenty of strong sun and rain which is fantastic for vegetation. Together with volcanic soils most plants do very well in this climate, to the point where the Californian Redwood tree grows three-times faster in New Zealand than where it originates.

Just as organic life grows rapidly when the environment is just right, so it is with our words – they create the environment for growth in our lives. Our speech and thought life has the ability to either empower or dis-empower the truth of God's word in our lives, because as a man thinks in his heart, so he is (Proverbs 23:7). Many of us would grow three-times as fast if we only learned the power of the tongue!

Deliverance from Slavery

The reason some of us still feel like we are in the spiritual wilderness, is not because of our circumstances, but because of our declarations! Our words are imprisoning us. As I was going to sleep one night, God said to me, 'Phil, deliverance from slavery is always proceeded by prophetic declaration.' I started to think about Moses standing before Pharaoh declaring 'let my people go'. It seemed the most unlikely of declarations in the circumstances. But like God, Moses' prophetic declarations created something in the visible world out of the spiritual world. He called into being something that did not exist and pretty soon slaves were walking free towards their promised land. This was more than the power of positive thinking. When we bring our thoughts and speech in line with Biblical reality and Holy Spirit revelation, the right kind of freedom is released in and through us. His Word in my mouth releases captives.

Walking the Neighbourhood

When my children were still young, my son went through months of chronic nightmares which created two sleep-deprived and desperate parents. His nightmares were so powerful that he couldn't go to sleep unless one of us was lying next to him holding his hand. We tried every prayer and parenting technique in the handbook, but to no avail, until one day, out of sheer exhaustion, I asked God for some kind of key that would bring breakthrough. I felt the Holy Spirit tell me to walk around our neighbourhood each night after dinner for six days and to declare His word, and then the breakthrough would come.

Willing to try anything at that stage (I even would have blown silver trumpets, like Joshua, if I thought it would help), I set off each night, praying and declaring breakthrough and peace over the neighbourhood. On the sixth night, Sam again woke up, having had a terrible nightmare, but instead of calling for us he decided to pray, and promptly went back to sleep. When asking him about it in the morning, he casually threw in, 'Yeah, I prayed and I heard God speak to me out loud from behind the curtain.'

'What did He say?' we both asked, amazed at what we were hearing.

'He just said, "Sam, think of me." So I did, and went to sleep.'

That broke months of sleeplessness and demonic dreams, which we later found out were probably the result of the curses of a lady deeply involved in the occult, but that's another story! The point is this: deliverance from slavery is always preceded by prophetic declaration.

When we speak to natural impossibilities with words of prophetic faith, the very things that exist in spiritual realms are enabled to become realities in the earthly. The rest that existed in God's world became rest in our world that night, because our words created a bridge between the two. Our words have power because we are created in our Daddy's image. Therefore, to create environments of prophetic health we need to learn to guard our tongues and speak words that bring life and not death.

Identifying and Overcoming Destructive Speech Habits

The apostle James, when writing about the power of speech, compares our words to a rudder on a ship or a bit that steers a horse, saying:

'Likewise, the tongue is a small part of the body, but it makes great boasts. Consider what a great forest is set on fire by a small spark. The tongue also is a fire, a world of evil among the parts of the body. It corrupts the whole body, sets the whole course of one's life on fire, and is itself set on fire by hell.' (James 3:5-6)

Those are some strong statements right there, and vital to pay attention to. I am amazed how many times I can be prophesying life over someone else and in the next breath can be speaking or thinking junk over myself. James says that those negative words have their origin in hell and can set my whole life on fire if I don't guard my tongue.

I remember in a particularly difficult season of life, as a reaction to the pressure I was feeling as a church leader and prophet, I would repeatedly say to Carole and myself, 'I think I'll just become a postman!' I have nothing against those who deliver mail for a living; it was purely my idea of a much simpler life and a way to escape. One day, the Lord rebuked me sternly and said, 'Phil, stop saying you are going to become a postman. That's not what I have called you to do. I called you to be a prophet, so get on and be one.' That was the end of that!

Prophets have to become a message as much as give a message, therefore identifying some of the common destructive speech habits and their antidotes is a crucial element in building a healthy prophetic culture. Let's consider a few of these together now.

1. Self-fulfilling Curses

I don't know about you, but I find it pretty easy to be negative about myself, and even call this a virtue. One of the peculiar traits of British culture is a highly developed system of self-deprecating humour where we basically put ourselves down in an effort to either make people laugh or not appear proud. The trouble is, so often the negative things we say about ourselves are not just things we say but actually believe, and our false humility ends up killing us from the inside out. If words become worlds, some of us are creating whole planets of insecurity, inferiority and ineptitude just through self-harming speech habits that neither honour God nor build us up. It has to stop!

More often than not, the negative words we say and think about ourselves come from the things we have heard significant others in our life say or not say. These words, unless brought into submission to the truth of God's opinion about us, can easily become so part of our belief system and of our own identity, that it is hard for many of us to disentangle fact from fiction, right from wrong.

I was raised in a home where I received high affirmation and love. My parents were, and continue to be, hugely encouraging, yet, despite this fact, I still walked through painful experiences outside of my family, which affected my view of myself. For many of my younger years at school I was bullied, not physically, but verbally. I often had bad eczema and dry skin, which of course is a magnet for every kid who wants to make someone else's life a misery. I remember one particular lad, whose nickname for me was Freddy, after Freddy Krueger, the gnarled up, ghoulish character in the movie *Nightmare on Elm Street* whose face was always scratched up and bleeding. While brushing it off at the time, these encounters bruised me very deeply.

The words and nicknames that came in my direction, created an insecurity and inability to believe in my own worth and attractiveness, which began to collide in my relationship with Carole when we first began dating. One famous evening, early in our courtship, I sat her down and said, 'I have to ask you an honest question. Do you want to be with me just because you know I will treat you well, respect and care for you, or do you actually fancy me and find me attractive as well?'

It was a question born from deep pain and a false belief about who I was. Praise the Lord, I discovered that day that I was indeed my wife's dream man and the rest is history, but it was a big moment for me. God has used Carole wonderfully to heal up a part of me that I never thought could be. Negative words in my past had created a roadblock in my present, which only loving truth could conquer.

So many prophetic people have become too accommodating and familiar with the old backing tracks, which play endlessly on a loop inside of their heads; thoughts such as 'I'm ugly. I'm no good. I'm a failure. I'm a disappointment. I'm a loser. I'm unattractive. I'm boring. I'm unwanted. I'm alone. I'm easily rejected. I'm unintelligent', churn around inside our brains, unchecked and unhindered. You can fill in your own blanks for the lies you are accommodating today.

These lies, when accommodated and reinforced by negative self-talk, can start to create and sustain demonic ecosystems in which we begin to live out and prove to ourselves the very things we fear are true. Psychology calls it self-fulfilling prophecy, but the Bible calls it a curse!

20th-century sociologist Robert K. Merton is the man credited with coining the expression 'self-fulfilling prophecy'. In his book *Social Theory and Social Structure*, Merton illustrates self-fulfilling prophecy with the following example: 'When Roxanna falsely believes her marriage will fail, her fears of such failure actually cause the marriage to fail.'[13]

In other words, a positive or negative declaration, declared as truth when it is actually false, may sufficiently influence people so that their reactions ultimately fulfil the once-false declaration. We become what we fear.

As James says, the whole course of our life gets set on fire, simply because we fail to recognise a lie from the truth. Self-fulfilling curses become like that rudder, steering the ship of our life in the wrong direction. Well, it's time to take the wheel back!

Giving Back Courage
One of the antidotes to self-fulfilling curses is to remember who you are and to suck up encouragement.

Encouragement, which we will talk about in more detail later in this book, is such a crucial input and output for prophetic people. The word 'encourage' originally comes from the French, which literally means to make one strong or daring or to put courage into someone. When we remember who we are and whose we are, we drink from the deepest well of encouragement we can find.

Godly encouragement reveals how the Lord really sees things from His perspective. It is more than just a happy thought, comforting word or arm around the shoulder, as good as those things are. Biblical encouragement actually inspires us to live as God now sees us – special treasures, a Holy people, redeemed, ambassadors and co-heirs with Christ. It gives us wings!

Once, when visiting a church overseas led by an incredibly faithful man of God, I took some time before the message to publicly honour and encourage him. I looked him in the eyes and publicly thanked him for his years of service, labour and sacrifice. I honoured him for his gifting, his love and his faithfulness. I then asked the entire congregation to stand and applaud their pastor and express their love for him. As the room stood and erupted in cheers and shouts lasting many minutes, tears streamed down his face as he drank in the pure water of godly encouragement. I wish I'd had a camera to capture that moment, because we saw something of God's estimate of his value and worth being imparted in a fresh way. It was beautiful, but that is how the power of godly encouragement works. It finds the treasure in people and puts it on display.

In our church staff meetings we spend some time encouraging those who have had birthdays that month. We take it in turns to pour in truth about who they are, what they mean to us and how valuable they are. Usually there is not a dry eye in the house. How different that kind of culture is to what most experience at home or the workplace. The church should be the encouragement capital of your town or city, because that is what God is like. One of the absolute keys to building a courageous prophetic church which stays together and kicks serious enemy butt is encouragement.

One of the very first exercises I regularly take people through when I am doing basic introductions to the prophetic is the power of encouragement. I pair people up, with the instruction that they are to encourage their partner 'assertively' by looking them in the eyes, laying a hand on their shoulder and speaking the truth of who they are and what they mean to you. Time and again, it's amazing how this simple tool instantly changes frosty atmospheres into those of life, expectancy and joy. It's easy to see the gaps, but a skill to spot the treasure in people!

Godly Self-talk

I can't underline enough how vital it is that you learn, not just to understand but repeat in your mind and with your mouth, what is now true. God says that you are fearfully and wonderfully made (Psalm 139:14). You cannot hate yourself and the way you look without offending the God who made you! God says that He has crowned you with glory and honour (Psalm 8:5). You cannot dishonour yourself without dishonouring Him! God says that you are His workmanship and work of art (Ephesians 2:10). You cannot tolerate undermining mindsets about your worth, without undermining your Father! The way you handle your own self-talk is actually, fundamentally, a worship issue. Your view of yourself reflects your view of the Father who gave you life, value and meaning.

Imagine Father God at the pottery wheel, His hands sculpting and moulding your life, like clay. He is crafting you into someone else's image and likeness, the image of His most beloved son, Jesus. When the pot starts to say 'I suck, I'm useless' it is really saying, 'God, You're useless and so is the model'. Knowing who you are in Christ is a worship issue, because when you behold the true majestic extent of His handiwork in your life, you cannot help but respond in praise. You bring glory to your Father when you honour yourself, just as He honours you.

2. Grumbling and Arguing

The apostle Paul nonchalantly throws in this instruction to the Philippians as he writes to them, saying, 'Do everything without grumbling or arguing' (Philippians 2:14). This is possibly among the most challenging things he ever penned, but it also reveals something of his understanding of our new creation in Christ. Thankfulness is our new home and gratefulness is our new native language.

Because prophetic people are anachronistic by nature, living as they do with a heightened awareness of future realities, they are sometimes thought to be some of the glummest people on the face of the whole darn planet! When present reality fails to match up with our revelation of what God wants to do in the future, impatience, frustration and grumbling can be the unhappy bedfellows of the prophet, which neither helps his or her cause, nor honours God. Prophets have to call God's people into the future, not through pessimism or complaining about today's circumstances but by optimistic prophesying about tomorrow's possibilities. Prophetic culture must always be infused with hope.

One of my favourite passages of Scripture is the account of Ezekiel in the valley of dry bones in Ezekiel chapter 37. If you were to read this passage of Scripture to me, I would probably cry on the spot, because it means that much to me; it offers us a great illustration of the kind of words we are called to speak when we face frustration and difficulty.

Ezekiel finds himself in the most unpromising place imaginable; a valley (symbolising a place of hardship) filled with a bunch of dead guys. In all likelihood, these dead guys are a defeated army and all that remains of them are, well, remains. This is just the sort of place I would complain about being in and, let's face it, you wouldn't have to look very far to find some friends to join you because misery loves company! It is amazing how grumblers always find one another. Grumbling has to be right up there as one of the most socially acceptable sins in the body of Christ today, but all grumbling does is fix us on the impossibility of our present circumstances. God has a much more radical plan for us! It is time to prophesy.

Ezekiel is called to prophesy life to the dead bones and to turn a valley of defeat into a vista of victory. Ezekiel is about to learn, as he prophesies to the bones and the breath, that God's words in his mouth have all the creative power of God's words in God's mouth. He is about to learn how to co-create with God.

A few years ago I was sitting in my lounge when my laptop suddenly powered down and would not start up again. Carole was quietly sitting in the corner reading while I pulled out every technological solution I could think of to get the thing back on again, but to no avail. Nothing was working and I was starting to panic. Twenty minutes passed, and still nothing. I was getting more and more agitated and began to complain. Quietly Carole asked whether I had prayed over it yet and declared God's word, to which I sheepishly replied, 'No, not yet dear!' I laid hands on the laptop, commanded it to work in Jesus' name and instantly it turned on! Prophetic words have great creative power and grumbling apparently none.

Paul, speaking about God's call to Abraham to become a father to many nations, even though he had no offspring yet, says: 'As it is written: "I have made you a father of many nations." He is our father in the sight of God, in whom he believed – the God who gives life to the dead and calls into being things that were not' (Romans 4:17).

Prophecy, in part, is calling into being things that were not. Prophecy does not just predict the future, it helps create it.

A few years ago, a young man came and found me and asked if I remembered prophesying over him, and after a short discussion I did. I had picked him out of the back of a meeting in the north of England and shared how I felt he was going to be used by God in the music business, playing the bass guitar, and that in a few years' time he would be cutting his own recording deals and playing in influential circles in the nation. I never got to meet him in person afterwards but now, years later, he found me in another part of England to share his story. He told me that the day I prophesied over him, he had just walked into the meeting and wasn't even meant to be there. As he walked in, I picked him out. At the time I was prophesying he had only just begun to learn the bass guitar and my words seemed far off for his stage of development. He shared how my words seemed to spark supernatural life in him and his growth just went exponential overnight. Within just a few years, he became such a proficient bass guitarist that he quickly made a living as a full-time session musician, playing in London's west-end and had recently toured with a very well-known UK pop act. As he spoke to me he was about to release his very first solo work. He thanked me for speaking words that created life in him. True biblical prophecy always empowers life, especially when those who hear God's words respond and take action.

This is why grumbling will never get you into your promised land, but only leave you in the wilderness. Our words can create negative spiritual ecosystems, where we start to live out the very negative things that we have complained about instead of prophesied faith over! To borrow Martin Luther King's great words, we are called to 'transform dark yesterdays into bright tomorrows,'[14] through words of prophetic faith which raise dead armies and herald the dawning of a new reformation in the nations. Yes it may be dark, but what better time to turn up the light and prophesy with faith. Speak to 'them bones'!

3. Accommodating Dark Thoughts

The third area we must bring under Christ's rule is our thoughts. Thoughts are the unspoken deeds of tomorrow and what we sow and allow to grow in our thought life, ultimately changes other lives and shapes the future. George Dana Boardman put it brilliantly when he said, 'Sow a thought, reap an act; sow an act, reap a habit; sow a habit, reap a character; sow a character, reap a destiny.' We always reap what we sow and it starts with our thought life. Destinies are birthed in the hidden place before they ever find the light of day.

When Paul starts to write about spiritual warfare to the Corinthians, he does not start by naming any prevailing principalities or calling believers to prayer and fasting. He starts by focusing on the battle between their ears. He says:

'For though we live in the world, we do not wage war as the world does. The weapons we fight with are not the weapons of the world. On the contrary, they have divine power to demolish strongholds. We demolish arguments and every pretension that sets itself up against the knowledge of God, and we take captive every thought to make it obedient to Christ.' (2 Corinthians 10:3-5)

Paul identifies the fact that the most intense warfare happens in the realm of arguments (literally reasonings), pretensions (literally lofty things or presumptions) and thoughts (the verdicts that come from using the mind), and that the believer has been equipped with special weapons to demolish these powers, and bring them into line with the truth.

The enemy of our souls is a liar by nature and the way that he steals, kills and destroys is simply by talking to us and getting us to believe the version of reality that he is selling. The only power he has is the power we give him when we agree with his False Evidence Appearing Real (aka FEAR).

A few years ago, I went through a strange few months when I lost motivation, energy and drive and began to believe the lie that I had made a mistake when I moved my family to Bedford, just a short time earlier. Thoughts plagued me from the moment I woke up: 'You've made a terrible mistake. You don't belong here. You have messed up your family. It's never going to work. Pack up and go home.' It was pretty intense and very persistent and I just assumed that these thoughts were my own, until one day God asked me to go and buy Kris Vallotton's excellent book, *Spirit Wars*.[15]

In it, Kris describes a moment in his life when he suddenly realised that not all his thoughts were his own. As I read that one line, everything instantly made sense. 'These thoughts are not my own – these are ideas and arguments from the pit,' I realised. As soon as I had been able to identify the source I was able to take action and authority over my little grey cells and bring my thoughts back into line with the truth.

When we pray with people who are facing big obstacles or

issues in their life we often ask, 'What is the lie that you are believing?' because our fear and shame often have their origin in thoughts that are not our own. Dismantling demonic fortresses starts with identifying what is false and believing what is true.

If you want to build a healthy prophetic culture where God's words take root and take ground, we have to learn to fight with the truth in our mouths. Practically this means regularly declaring what is true to yourself and others. It means creating an environment where friends and family can rebuke you for believing nonsense and instead encourage you to remember right realities. It means steeping yourself in God's word and allowing Scripture to wash your brain with clear, cool, liquid heavenly thinking. It means creating space for the ultimate revealer, the Holy Spirit, to encounter you, fill you and open up to you the wonder of your new creation reality in Christ. Paul says that the Spirit 'we have received is not the spirit of the world, but the Spirit who is from God, so that we may understand what God has freely given us' (1 Corinthians 2:12). The beautiful and wonderful person of the Spirit is the ultimate unveiler of truth concerning your identity in Christ. Receiving the Spirit is the chief business of a strong prophetic culture, because it illuminates what is now true, and truth always brings freedom!

Your words have very great power because you are created in the image of your Father in heaven. Speak and think words that release life, not death, and the prophetic will thrive and flourish, because God's word, honoured in both your mouth and your mind, will reproduce that same honour in the environment and culture around you.

Notes:

13. http://nlpnotes.com/self-fulfilling-prophecy/

14. http://www.notable-quotes.com/k/king_jr_martin_luther.html

15. http://www.amazon.co.uk/Spirit-Wars-Winning-Invisible-Against-ebook/dp/B006N55TP2

Chapter Eight:
Holy Spirit Order
Learning to Let Revelation Flow in Public Worship

It was a typical Sunday morning, like many others before. One of my good friends stood and began to prophesy over a couple that were visiting that day. He began by pointing to the lady, saying, 'I see a picture of a red door and the number 42 written over it and you are kicking the door down. God says He has seen your faith and heard your prayers and breakthrough is coming. Does that mean anything to you?!'

Struggling to keep the tears from flowing, the lady began to tell how she had started to work at a predominantly Muslim school and had been praying for God to use her and bring breakthrough, but she had started to lose hope. The door to the staff-room was red and there were exactly 42 staff members! Suddenly, God had kindled fresh faith in her heart in the midst of the church family worshipping together. It was a beautiful moment – one of awe and wonder in corporate worship. I could tell many other stories like this.

The reality is, churches put on display what they most value on Sunday mornings. Sundays are still the shop window for the values we hold dear and the virtues we want to perpetuate. My great concern is that many churches have become embarrassed about the prophetic in public, and have solely relegated it to the sidelines of hidden gatherings, when it is designed to release kingdom life in powerful ways, as described in the story I've related.

Smith Wigglesworth wrote in his book *Ever Increasing Faith,* 'Wherever the Holy Ghost has right of way, the gifts of the Spirit will be in manifestation; and where these gifts are never in manifestation, I question whether He is present.'

The apostle Paul expected that whenever we come together, we would have an opportunity to receive and hear Holy Spirit inspired revelation. He writes to the Corinthians saying:

'What then shall we say, brothers? When you come together, everyone has a hymn, or a word of instruction, a revelation, a tongue or an interpretation. All of these must be done for the strengthening of the church. If anyone speaks in a tongue, two – or at the most three – should speak, one at a time, and someone must interpret. If there is no interpreter, the speaker should keep quiet in the church and speak to himself and God. Two or three prophets should speak, and the others should weigh carefully what is said. And if a revelation comes to someone who is sitting down, the first speaker should stop. For you can all prophesy in turn so that everyone may be instructed and encouraged. The spirits of prophets are subject to the control of prophets. For God is not a God of disorder but of peace.' (1 Corinthians 14:26-33)

Paul says to this spiritually alive, if somewhat chaotic and immature church, that whenever they come together there will be singing, teaching, prophetic revelation, speaking in tongues and interpretation. Paul's point is not that we create a liturgy, but that we have life. This is not a prescriptive methodology but a Holy Spirit inspired doxology. The Holy Spirit is a river, not a stagnant pool. He is flowing somewhere. The point of this teaching to the Corinthians is that we learn to flow prophetically with what the Holy Spirit is doing, and thereby get life. Paul says if the prophetic is handled well, it will result in the strengthening of the church (v26).

Learning how to flow by Holy Spirit revelation brings strength, not weakness to our corporate gatherings, if only we will take time to learn how to do this well. Let's consider how we actually go about doing that.

1. Dynamic Direction

Summarising his teaching on public worship Paul makes the following statement:

'Therefore, my brothers and sisters, be eager to prophesy, and do not forbid speaking in tongues. But everything should be done in a fitting and orderly way. (1 Corinthians 14:39-40)

Now, I like order as much as the next man, but I can't help wondering if Paul's sense of 'fitting and orderly' was somewhat different from the idea many of us have in Western cultures. The word 'fitting' here means what is respectable, honourable and 'having good form', and the word 'order' simply means properly arranged or appointed. Paul's encouragement is less about neatness, and much more about well-ordered life. When the prophetic is expressed in a corporate setting, it should be done in an honourable and well-arranged way and it should bring life.

For the prophetic to truly strengthen the Church in the way God intends, it has to avoid man-made chaos and embrace Holy Spirit order. Holy Spirit order, in my opinion, is much more like a fast-flowing river than a set of train tracks. Train-track 'meetings' are very rigid, prescriptive, predictable and pre-planned. You know which way you are going to go. It is safe but potentially dull. A river 'meeting' however, rushes powerfully with the ebb and flow of the tide, rising and falling, lilting and lulling as the currents surge towards the open mouth of the sea. Rivers still have a very clear sense of direction, but operate with a whole different set of dynamic principles. This is what Holy Spirit order is like. When we operate out of deference to His leadership in our public gatherings, we can always guarantee life, power, flow and dynamic direction.

This 'dynamic-direction' principle is underlined by Paul when he gives some specific instruction on how prophets should work together in a public worship setting, saying, 'Two or three prophets should speak, and the others should weigh carefully what is said. And if a revelation comes to someone who is sitting down, the first speaker should stop. For you can all prophesy in turn so that everyone may be instructed and encouraged' (1 Corinthians 14:29-31).

The prophet's job is not to get his or her voice heard, but to make sure that His voice is clearly heard. The sense here is that the second prophet is adding revelation in the flow of what the first has already kicked off. It is not one prophet prophesying about one subject and then another prophesying on something completely different. They are adding revelation and adding value to one another because they are in the same dynamically flowing river! It is heading in the same direction.

By working together in humility, in team and with a deferential attitude, prophetic people in dynamic partnership can help the people catch what God is saying in that particular moment in time. This is what Holy Spirit 'order' looks and feels like. Prophets add progressive revelation as God gives it, and this is all part of communicating a cohesive message which brings peace, not confusion, to those listening.

I have been in far too many charismatic churches over the years where I have seen the exact opposite of this Pauline model – where prophetic ministry has less resembled a well-ordered dynamic moment, and much more closely resembled a free for all or a monkeys' tea party. By the time the tenth person has shared their favourite prophetic thought for the day, you have not only lost the will to listen but you cannot even remember what the first person said. Instead of dreaming with God we are dreaming of Sunday lunch. This kind of model only causes us to despise the very thing we actually want, which is to hear God clearly together in a dynamic and meaningful way.

It is entirely possible to prophesy ourselves out of the anointing rather than into it, to the point where no-one really knows what is going on, least of all our poor guests and visitors.

I find it interesting that in Acts 11:27 we read that when a group of prophets came down from Jerusalem to Antioch, all of them could have prophesied but only one did. Agabus stood on behalf of them all and predicted that a severe famine would hit the Roman world. It was about prophetic quality, not quantity. The spirit of prophets is subject to the control of prophets – meaning we exercise self-control, because the goal is not that you catch my heart, but that we catch His heart together.

Presence-fuelled Principles

One of the great principles restored to the Church during the charismatic renewal was that of body ministry and the priesthood of all believers. This led to meetings that were much more open and participative, where spiritual gifts were exercised. No longer was spiritual inspiration confined to the paid pastor, but was available to all who were filled with the Spirit. This is a beautiful principle that must be held onto.

There is a danger, however, that this can still create nothing more than a new kind of charismatic liturgy devoid of the life of the Spirit, if operating on principle rather than an awareness of, and sensitivity to, His presence.

Our principle is, 'we want contributions in our meetings', and therefore if we have a couple of prophecies, a reading and a blessed thought, we think we have had a good meeting full of the Spirit. Well, not necessarily. Principle alone will not get you to life. We must learn to flow and become sensitive to the leading of His presence, rather than rigidly applying the principle. I do want contributions in our meetings, but only if they actually help pull us deeper into God's glory and presence.

The practical effect of this truth in our Sunday services is that we will often turn away people who come forward with a prophetic word, not because they are necessarily wrong, but because we as meeting hosts and leaders do not feel it will take us deeper into God's presence.

This doesn't mean that we don't experiment, learn on the job and have some great heroic failures along the way. We are not perfectionists but a family. But the goal of the prophetic is always to catch the flow of the river and prophesy from that place.

Now I want to move on to some practicalities; how, in our prophesying, we can be most effective in flowing with the presence of God and bringing strength to a meeting with the revelations and contributions we bring.

2. Shaping Words

Imagine a typical Sunday morning. You arrive at church, settle into your seat and begin to worship God. Suddenly, thoughts begin forming and you realise that God may be speaking to you and want you to prophesy. What you do at this juncture is absolutely critical and can be the difference between bringing something which genuinely brings help and strength or something that is just part of the background noise of the morning.

In a prophetic culture, people learn to ask questions of the revelation they are receiving. God is not averse to dialogue and processing, because in my experience prophetic words rarely come fully formed. They come as divinely planted seeds which need nurturing. Note how many times the prophets of Scripture ask supplementary questions of the Lord!

Often we can be so overjoyed at having a word that we leap into action before asking God what to do with the things He has already begun to share with us. Relationship and intimacy is the very best context for growing in revelation, because God loves to talk to His friends.

Often words from God need to go through a process of filtration where they are shaped in our hearts. God speaking in a moment in time does not necessarily mean that He wants you to share that word immediately or in its current form. Some words are like a good cup of tea; the tea bag needs to stay in the cup for a decent amount of time before you take it out. Let God's words brew a while in your heart before you offer them to others.

Words have an appointed time and sometimes God's instruction may be to 'seal it up' till the right moment (see Daniel 12:4). In a prophetic culture, certain questions become critical to help us judge timing and content.

a. Ask, Does it Add Anything?

This is crucial as you start shaping a word to bring it publicly. Prophesies are meant to be laced with 'revelation' as Paul describes (1 Corinthians 14:26). The word 'revelation' means to unveil, uncover or reveal. In other words, prophecies should genuinely have something to say that is hidden unless you disclose it! These revelations can be about God's character, God's present purposes or His future plans. Prophecy is not a blessed thought but an unveiling.

Often the words we receive are descriptions, rather than revelations. I remember one Sunday when the Holy Spirit was moving quite powerfully, a lady came to me as I was leading the meeting and shared a picture. She saw Holy Spirit bubbles rising up from the ground and into the heavens. Her application was to encourage people that God was really moving powerfully that morning and to engage with Him.

I thanked her and encouraged her that what she had seen was a great description of what was already happening. I did not let her share the word publicly because it was not revelatory and did not add anything to what God was already up to. People were already meeting with Jesus, and her description of this was a great private confirmation of what we knew and could sense.

b. Ask, Is it For Everyone, Someone or Myself?

God shares these things with us because He loves to talk to

His friends, especially those who take the time to listen. But this doesn't mean it is necessarily for public consumption. In a prophetic culture we learn to ask the question, 'Is this for everyone, someone or myself?'

There is an intrinsic joy in God speaking to us. He likes to talk. Sometimes He just speaks because He is friendly. He shares secrets with us and whispers truth to us. The words that we share are very often for ourselves more than others.

Likewise, some prophecies are not for the microphone, but for someone specific near us. When we train our prophetic teams, we deliberately get them to engage with God about who He wants to speak to in any given context. On one such occasion, we challenged everyone to write down a prophetic word on a blank postcard, which they would later give someone in the evening meeting. We all wrote down what we felt God was saying. In the evening we then loitered with intent, asking God to give us an exact match with the things we had already written. One of our team approached a young man, gave the card and began to share what was on it. It contained some quite detailed descriptions of the kind of scientific career the young man would go into and how God was going to provide, all of which was true and brought huge blessing and encouragement.

On another occasion, my family and I were visiting a highly prophetic church in the United States. My children were about to embark on a week-long 'school of worship', where we knew nobody. Before arriving we had specifically prayed that God would connect us to children the same age as ours and that we would get invited back to lunch at someone's house. After the first Sunday service we attended was over, a lady approached us with a napkin in her hand. She went on to explain how God had spoken to her during the service to invite us back for lunch. In case we said yes, she had drawn a map to her house on the back of the napkin. What was even more amazing, was that this lady turned out to be a leader at the school of worship and had children exactly the same age as ours and knew some of our English friends!

In a prophetic culture, people ask good questions of the words they receive – is it for myself, someone else or everybody?

c. Ask, Am I Responding to the Corporate Mood?

Prophetic people are typically 'feelers'. This means they are highly sensitive to atmospheres and moods, whether that is in McDonald's or a Sunday service. Consequently, we can easily bring prophetic words or exhortations which seek to counter-balance the corporate mood in the room, rather than from genuine third-heaven revelation.

For example, many of us will have felt those moments in church when everyone just seems, well, more than a little apathetic, tired and lethargic. The corporate mood is crying out 'We're tired and can't be bothered!' In reaction to this, prophetic people can easily prophesy to correct this, rather than deliver what God is actually saying.

The best way to shift corporate atmospheres is not reaction, but revelation.

I remember well when my kids were very small, that the answer to their bad or moody behaviour was not always a rebuke, but a welcome distraction. So often the key to snatching them up out of tetchiness was not a lecture on being better behaved, but fresh focus on a different stimulus or truth. 'Look at that robin in the garden! Who wants to go to the park and play? How high can you jump? Who wants to know a secret?!' The right revelation or question would often shift their perspective far more than a reaction to immature behaviour.

The same is true in church. Genuine prophetic ministry shifts our focus onto what is really important and enables us to come into line with what God is saying from the throne-room. A message of 'Come on you lot, get your act together and worship like you mean it. After all, Jesus died on a cross for you!' is unlikely to do any more than produce guilt or rebellion. Ask yourself, what is God actually wanting to say this morning, and avoid reactive prophetic contributions rooted in negative emotion rather than timely prophetic truth.

3. Judging Timing

Once you have asked these questions and have concluded it is for everyone, then comes the question of getting your timing right. Now, this is definitely not an exact science and requires a lot of trial and error. It is crucial that you don't let fear rob you of the adventure of having a go and learning some lessons on the journey. I recently taught a message entitled 'Failure is an option; timidity is not' which captures the attitude I think we should adopt. The only way to learn is to try! Here are some comments on getting timing right.

a. Avoid Insecurity

Often our insecurities can cause us to leap before it is time. Early on in my prophetic journey I often shared out of the insecurity of needing to be heard, rather than because it strengthened the church. We must learn to kill our insecure inclinations. I don't prophesy to be accepted – I am accepted, therefore whether I prophesy or not, I am loved. If you are prophesying for affirmation, God is exposing a heart issue that needs healing and mending. We prophesy from affirmation, knowing we are already God's favourites, whether we are heard or not!

b. Make Enjoying God a Top Priority

The main deal of our worship times is that God is glorified and enjoyed. A successful corporate church meeting is one where Jesus is put at the centre, is adored, thanked, welcomed and honoured. That is top priority. Therefore, don't cut across that primary purpose with a man-centred word! The highest form of prayer and prophecy is praise. God is enthroned on the praises of His people. There is a corporate prophesying going on when we worship together that is broadcast on heavenly radio waves to principalities and rulers of the invisible world. The Church is God's corporate prophetic word of what He is doing on the earth, uniting people from diverse backgrounds, stories, colours, shapes and sizes and making them one in Christ. The demons quake when we honour Christ as one new man. Make it a priority to get lost and immersed in God.

For this reason, I rarely allow a public contribution too early in a meeting, unless it is God focused or inspires us to worship more.

c. Lean into Others

The sense I get from 1 Corinthians 14 is that prophets were meant to be working together to share revelation that benefitted the Church. One of the best aids when you are unsure about when to bring a word publicly is to share your thoughts with someone else who can help. For this reason, many of our key prophetic people will sit near to or next to each other, so that they can bounce ideas off one another. I think part of the weighing aspect of leadership is that we can help carry the issue of timing together. I help facilitate a team of prophets at a large festival in the UK, whose remit is to help catch the prophetic flow of what God is doing at the event and discern timing together. If you are anywhere near us in those settings, you will see a whole host of conversations going on, as we share burdens, revelations and insights from the Lord. This is such a helpful model in getting the timing right. Together we can catch the flow.

d. Jump Through 'the Window'

There is often a moment in God which I call 'the window'. The window is that unseen but nevertheless tangible moment in God when it is right to go for it and share a contribution. Often the window is only open for 5-10 seconds and it needs to be jumped through right there and then.

In our Sunday gatherings it is the meeting leader who decides when that window is open and when to pass the microphone to those who have already shared privately in their ear during the worship time. It just takes experience and sensitivity to the Spirit to know when to jump in at the right moment and it is not an exact science! Learning sensitivity to His presence is the best training ground for judging those God-given moments with increasing accuracy and effect.

e. Air-traffic Control

As a meeting leader, it will not be uncommon to have 5-6 people come and share with me that they have words to bring. At this moment I have to ask, which order is going to release most life and which contributions are the most anointed in this moment? You don't have to share them in the order that they came to you, because the goal is not fairness, but life. Sometimes you will feel like air-traffic control, as you literally 'rack them, stack them and pack them', deciding which plane to bring in to land first. For this reason, I believe the best hosts of public meetings tend to be those who carry a strong prophetic intuition alongside a strong leadership gifting. You have to be able to hear God for yourself and have the leadership to govern diligently and bring people with you.

4. Delivering the Words

There are two great keys to delivering well what God has given you to share publicly: clarity and charisma.

Clarity

You could have the greatest prophetic revelation in the world, but if no-one can understand what on earth you are saying it will benefit no-one. Clarity will be massively helped if you speak like yourself and not like a version of King James English from the 17th century. You will also be helped by simple things like good microphone technique and clear diction.

I was once in another nation with a friend where we were ministering to a number of churches and leaders. After one week we had visited seven different churches, interacted with two apostolic networks, slept in seven different beds, travelled over 1,200 miles in the car and prophesied to over 100 individuals. It was intense. One of the pleasures of that trip was seeing my friend grow in his prophetic gifting and confidence, to the point where during one meal time, he began to prophesy over the girl sitting opposite him.

He said, 'I believe you are a singer but your microphone technique is not very good. During rehearsals the sound guys are always asking you to put the microphone closer to your mouth and speak clearer. This is really important because God wants your voice to be heard because you are a prophetic mouthpiece for His purposes.' She looked stunned and immediately confirmed that what he had prophesied was true. It was such a cool moment, but also illustrates what is true when we deliver words publicly. Hold the microphone to your mouth like a lollipop and speak confidently in your own voice and with a passion and dignity befitting a child of the King! He wants your voice to be heard.

Charisma

Secondly, prophesy with anointing. It was Smith Wigglesworth who said that he never dared to prophesy unless there was fire in it.[16] Simply put, when you are under the influence of the Spirit you prophesy freer, better and more effectively. When I attended my first ever training session in another church on treasure hunting, which is basically prophetic evangelism on the streets, the training instructor started with these immortal words: 'The best way to treasure hunt is this. Get drunk in the Spirit, stay drunk and get someone else drunk. That's it.' My kids immediately turned to me with shock written all over their little faces as if to say, is that allowed?!

Now, I'm not a massive fan of drinking language when it comes to the Spirit, because it tends to turn our understanding of the Spirit into a substance or force, not a relational God who we can know. However, the point was well made. The best way to prophesy effectively is to be filled to overflowing with the Spirit of God. That's when you prophesy best.

I pray that we will increasingly learn how to prophesy in a way that is not just ticking the boxes of charismatic theological principle, but in a way that powerfully reveals God's heart and transforms us. May God place a fresh fire in the heart of His prophets and let them burn brightly with the glory of His presence once again.

The effect of genuine God-anointed, well-timed and well-led prophetic ministry should be the flowing of the river of God's presence. Order in God's Kingdom means life, and a prophetic culture understands how to flow with God to bring about what He desires among His people. When Jesus cast the demons out of Legion it was orderly, but in a heavenly way. When Jesus threw the money changers' tables over, it was orderly in a heavenly way. When the Holy Spirit came on Cornelius' house as Peter was still speaking and they all began to prophesy, it was very orderly, but in a very heavenly way. The prophetic releases life!

Surely God is Among You!

As we come in to land, I'll share one example of how this happened in a church I was visiting. I had spent the first part of the weekend teaching and prophesying and I could feel the temperature of expectation rising as we headed into Sunday morning. As I began to prophesy about God's power to heal the sick, two young girls came running in at that very moment from their groups to share that Jesus had just healed them.

Their story of breakthrough led to more, as is often the case. Two ladies were healed of sinus problems, one of long-standing lower back pain, one of the after-effects of a broken ankle that had led to ligament damage, and one man felt significant improvement in his asthma! It was a beautiful time.

On top of this, two young men gave their lives to Christ that morning, having seen the demonstration of God's power in the church. One of them described how in the worship time he could feel heat and fire going up his arms, so he started to raise them like everyone else, even though he was not yet a believer. After opening his heart to Jesus, he told us that he had come that morning as an atheist, but was leaving a Christian. God was showing off His supernaturally abundant goodness and it was amazing to see.

Stories like that demonstrate why we must fight for biblical expressions of prophetic ministry in our public gatherings that really do 'reveal the secrets of their hearts' and cause them to exclaim, 'Surely God is among you!' It is time to get in the river and catch the flow again.

Notes:
16. *Ever Increasing Faith,* Smith Wigglesworth, Gospel Publishing House.

Chapter Nine:
God's Secret Weapon
The Son of Encouragement

A sure-fire hallmark of a truly prophetic culture is the beautiful and powerful presence of encouragement. No book on prophetic culture would be complete without a focus on this. Many have personified this through the years, but one particularly remarkable moment in my life brought home how precious and supernatural this gift really is.

A Heavenly Encounter

At the age of eighteen I was preparing to leave home for the first time and embark on a year-long internship at a church in Missouri, USA. While I was excited about the adventure I was also more than a little apprehensive. I was young, pretty green behind the ears, and had only just learnt to wash my own socks. In fact, that last line may not even be true.

Two months prior to leaving, I signed up to do a week-long evangelism team in the great city of Newcastle upon Tyne, where I would later move as a student, get my first job, start a family and lead in a church. Throughout the week I could not stop thinking about the great change my life was about to take. 'America! I'm moving to America! What am I doing?' To say I was feeling daunted would be an understatement. But one morning in that week stands out still for me, because a heavenly experience changed my perspective completely and released the power of prophetic encouragement into my life.

It was a twenty-minute walk to the church building from

the house I was staying in and, as I stepped out that morning, a girl standing across the other side of the street greeted me, arms waving above her head. She looked like a typical English student of a similar age to me, but I didn't recognise her. She called out my name and said, 'Are you going to the church? I'll walk with you.'

Thinking she must be a team member I'd not yet met, I agreed and we began the short journey together. 'So, what's about to happen in your life?' she asked me straightaway. I began to tell her about my imminent move abroad and all the things I would be involved in. As soon as I had finished, quite surprisingly, she began a nonstop, fifteen-minute barrage of encouragement that left me feeling ten-feet tall by the time she had finished. She spoke into every area that I was anxious about and poured truth onto it. It was as if she knew exactly how I was feeling in my heart and exactly what I needed to hear. My fears began to evaporate under the power of her words.

As we approached the church building she suddenly stopped and said to me, 'I have to be going now. I'm sure I'll see you later.' Saying our goodbyes, she went one way and I went the other. It was the last time I would see her. She never reappeared and no-one in the church knew who she was or anyone who even matched her description. I can only assume she was an angel, sent by the Lord to encourage me precisely in the moment I needed it most. I learnt that day that encouragement truly is the language of heaven.

Encouragement is the core, the essence of prophetic culture and is the greenhouse for growing big people who change the world. When we learn to encourage we create environments in which God is present in a powerful way. Notice the apostle Paul's exhortation and the promise it contains: 'Finally, brothers and sisters, rejoice! Strive for full restoration, encourage one another, be of one mind, live in peace. And the God of love and peace will be with you' (2 Corinthians 13:11).

Experiencing God's presence is directly connected to the way in which we relate to one another. When we create cultures built on heaven's DNA, we invite the one who inhabits heaven itself to draw near.

Sons and Daughters of Encouragement

When the apostle is writing about the essence of the prophetic, he makes this summary statement to the Christians in Corinth: 'But the one who prophesies speaks to people for their strengthening, encouraging and comfort' (1 Corinthians 14:3). The Greek word used for encouragement in this verse is *paraklesis*, which means 'an intimate urging or call that someone personally gives to deliver God's verdict'.[17] When we choose to encourage, we are speaking prophetically into people's lives of the very way God views things from His divine vantage point. When God's children encourage one another they are speaking their new native language.

One of the central characters in the early church was Barnabas, a man whose nickname was 'son of encouragement' (Acts 4:36). This nickname is not actually a linear translation of his name, but more of a paraphrase used by Luke, the writer of the book of Acts, to describe the kind of man Barnabas was.

The literal meaning of his name reveals something very interesting, however. The name Barnabas is made up of two key Aramaic elements, consisting firstly of *bar*, meaning son, and the second, *nebi*, meaning prophet. The Aramaic and Hebrew use of the word 'son', can mean either someone's offspring or, as it is more often applied, indicating that this member of a group possesses a certain skill or vocation.[18] The phrase 'son of the prophet', therefore, seems to indicate that the name 'Barnabas' literally means 'the prophet'.

My personal opinion is that Barnabas started out as the key prophet of the New Testament, and only later transitioned to a more apostolic role as the Church grew and developed (Acts 14:14). The core hallmark of Barnabas' prophetic ministry was encouragement, and when the apostle Paul later wrote about prophecy to the Corinthians I believe he had his friend Barnabas in mind. His prophetic encouragement was the model Paul wanted to see perpetuated in the Church. Paul had experienced first-hand the *paraklesis* that came through this man. Barnabas was a prophet who comforted, strengthened and encouraged God's people and created a vibrant prophetic culture wherever he went. To be a prophet is to be a son or daughter of encouragement.

An Encouragement Master-class: Barnabas and Paul

As we delve into this subject further, we are going to consider the special relationship Barnabas had with the apostle Paul. Their friendship has much to tell us about the true nature of biblical encouragement and how we can build this beautiful prophetic characteristic into the very fabric of our lives.

Barnabas presents us with a biblical master-class in how to encourage well. Without his encouragement, especially to the apostle Paul, the mighty advance of the gospel we read of in the New Testament may never have happened.

So what exactly did Barnabas do to earn his nickname 'son of encouragement' and how did he personally encourage his friend Paul?

1. Boasting About People's Strengths in the Presence of Others

The apostle Paul, while still known by his Jewish name Saul, has a dramatic conversion on the Damascus road and then proceeds to spend the next three years in Arabia (Galatians 1:18). Paul does not interact with the other apostles in Jerusalem until Barnabas finds him and initiates the introductions. Barnabas becomes the broker of apostolic relationships through his prophetic ministry. The way in which he goes about this is fascinating and instructive:

'But Barnabas took him and brought him to the apostles. He told them how Saul on his journey had seen the Lord and that the Lord had spoken to him, and how in Damascus he had preached fearlessly in the name of Jesus.' (Acts 9:27)

Barnabas gives us our first lesson in encouragement by deliberately boasting about Saul's strengths and courage in the presence of the other apostles. It is Barnabas who tells them how fearless Saul has been in his defence and preaching of the gospel. Essentially, he begins to brag about Saul. 'This guy is amazing! You wouldn't believe how courageous and fearless this man is. He is the real deal!' He acts as if he is Saul's biggest fan and most enthusiastic advocate.

This is a master class in encouragement, because there is nothing so uplifting as someone else acknowledging and calling out your brilliance and beauty in front of others. So often our encouragement to others is intensely personal, delivered in a very secret or individual way, which is great and has its place. But there is something so powerful about calling out the greatness in someone, by doing it publicly on full display for others to see.

A few years before we moved to Bedford to be part of the King's Arms Church, Carole and I visited the church as guest speakers for a leaders' weekend away. We were still living in the north-east of England at the time and were excited to spend some time serving our friends. Little did we know that our visit would profoundly change us as much as it would change them, but that part of the story is for another day!

On the Friday evening, before we were due to get up and speak for the first time, we were introduced to everyone by the meeting host in such glowing terms that I hardly recognised myself!

'Phil and Carole are a world-changing, culture-shaping couple who carry incredible anointing. They come to us as prophets, steeped in the grace of God and full of the power of the Spirit. . .'

and so it went on! I could hardly wait to hear myself speak. As we were then invited to stand, the whole room stood and cheered and applauded like we were returning war heroes. I felt truly humbled and stunned.

I also felt something rising up deep within my soul to be the person that matched the description just given. Consequently, the ministry that whole weekend was of the level I had never known before. The breakthroughs were powerful! Someone who took the trouble to look inside and encourage me in the presence of others had managed to pull something out of me I didn't even know was in there. They were calling out the treasure in me. Never had I felt quite so encouraged and honoured, both for who I was and who God was calling me to become.

It has since become one of my favourite pastimes to brag about people in the presence of others, because recognition always brings reward. When we take the time to recognise who people are in front of others, we create a climate of honour in which our encouragements become prophecies, and our prophecies become realities.

2. Recognise People by the Spirit Not the Flesh

Having met the apostles in Jerusalem, Saul returns home and spends his next 10 years back in Damascus living in relative obscurity while God reveals to him the mystery of the gospel through a series of divine encounters (Galatians 1:11-12; 2 Corinthians 12:1-4). We know little else about this particular decade in his life but God is preparing him for his future calling as apostle to the Gentiles.

Barnabas, in the mean time, is sent by the Jerusalem elders to Antioch where an extraordinary revival is taking place. Barnabas arrives and immediately sees evidence of the grace of God at work and begins to do what he does best – encourage (Acts 11:23). He also makes a bold move, which no-one else had apparently thought about. He goes to fetch Saul to invite him to be part of the team.

'Then Barnabas went to Tarsus to look for Saul, and when he found him, he brought him to Antioch. So for a whole year Barnabas and Saul met with the church and taught great numbers of people.' (Acts 11:25-26)

Barnabas remembered Saul. He had seen something in Saul that others had not. He believed in Saul and took the trouble and effort to call out what he saw.

Barnabas teaches us that encouragement is not always based upon what you can see with the naked eye, but what you perceive with spiritual insight. We need to learn that encouragement is not just performance based but prophetically driven. Calling out prophetic destiny sometimes means believing in people before they even believe in themselves.

As a fearful Gideon threshed wheat in a winepress, the angel of the Lord says, 'The LORD is with you, mighty warrior' (Judges 6:12). Now, either the angel had just got in touch with his sarcastic sense of humour or something much more profound was taking place. The angel was not mocking him but speaking prophetically. This was God's perspective on Gideon. Underneath all that timidity there was a valiant leader waiting to be encouraged into life.

This is exactly what Jesus does with Simon Peter in the seminal prophetic moment of that disciple's life. Jesus looks at Peter and calls out what he sees within him:

'And I tell you that you are Peter, and on this rock I will build my church, and the gates of Hades will not overcome it. I will give you the keys of the kingdom of heaven; whatever you bind on earth will be bound in heaven, and whatever you loose on earth will be loosed in heaven.' (Matthew 16:18-19)

I am pretty sure that those listening to that particular prophetic word may have wondered if Jesus had got that one wrong, because Peter was anything but a 'rock'. Peter suffered from what I would affectionately call 'foot in mouth disease'. He was impulsive, passionate, reckless and, with a sword in his hand, given to cutting off ears in defence of Jesus! He was anything but stable, secure, solid, dependable or rock-like.

Yet Jesus brings prophetic encouragement that is not rooted in his performance or personality, but in the destiny of God for his life. Jesus is drawing out the man Peter was called to be, not who he currently was.

There is more to you than meets the eye and sometimes what we need most is a prophetic encourager to perceive it and draw it out. One of the things I have noticed in myself is that I often have faith for people far sooner than others around me. My tendency is to promote people early and give opportunities that may seem premature to others. At the root of that tendency is a prophetic gift that recognises spiritual identity before outward appearance. Paul needed Barnabas to draw out who he really was. Most of us are only one Barnabas away from stepping into our God-given potential.

Part of growing in spiritual intelligence is learning to recognise the favour that someone else carries and to give honour accordingly. Barnabas saw something in Saul that drew him from the shadows and into the light – out of the stands and onto the pitch. How desperately we need this gift alive and well today.

3. Going Out of Your Way

Some of the most meaningful moments of encouragement come when others go deliberately out of their way, sometimes at great personal cost, to build us up.

The Bible nonchalantly recounts that Barnabas 'went to Tarsus to look for Saul' (Acts 11:25) in order to bring him to Antioch. In the days of bullet trains and motorways it is easy to forget that this was no mean feat for someone living in the first-century Mediterranean world. A round trip from Antioch to Tarsus was somewhere in the region of 170 miles and would have been undertaken on foot or donkey. At an average of 15 miles per day, in hot weather and an unforgiving desert region, you would not get much change out of 11 to 12 days travel. Barnabas' encouragement was very physical, tangible and costly and meant all the more because of it.

Truly prophetic cultures will be full of seen and unseen acts of physical, costly encouragements such as these, which communicate the honour and value God has for His sons and daughters.

A few years ago, my family had begun to pray, secretly, for an iPad. We certainly could not afford one at the time and while it was neither a necessity nor a need, we simply brought our requests to God and waited to see what would happen. One morning, a few months later, a young man walked into my office and announced that he had a gift to give my family. He placed his bag on the table and I thought to myself, 'This is so lovely. He is going to give us chocolate or sweets. How thoughtful!' Instead, he proceeded to pull out his iPad which he had bought earlier that year and handed it over. He said, 'For three months now God has been telling me to give you my iPad. I want to give it as a gift to your whole family as a sign of how much I love you, appreciate you and how much God loves you.'

I was blown away, both by his generosity but also the kindness of God. Tangible encouragement came through a physical moment that cost that man more than just words. When we encourage we must learn, at times, to go the extra mile to express how God views and values people. Be tactile, go out of your way, look people in the eyes, write cards, paint pictures, give away money, send flowers, call round the house and buy gifts. Use all the resources at your disposal to call out greatness in others and just watch what the Lord will do!

4. Courage Buddies: Fighting Battles Together

Paul and Barnabas fought battles side by side. Encouragement sometimes involves giving courage to one another to fight battles we cannot win on our own. The Christian life was never meant to be an individual pursuit but a team sport. We win together. Some battles can only be won with a courage buddy right by your side. Barnabas was such a man for the apostle Paul.

At a crucial juncture for the continued spread of the gospel, Paul and Barnabas get involved in a hot dispute over whether or not non-Jewish converts needed to get circumcised. The two of these men blazed a trail for the gospel of grace by arguing before the leaders in Jerusalem that God did not require new believers to submit to the outward sign of circumcision and obedience to Jewish law; it was faith in Christ alone which was enough to be saved.

'This brought Paul and Barnabas into sharp dispute and debate with them. So Paul and Barnabas were appointed, along with some other believers, to go up to Jerusalem to see the apostles and elders about this question.' (Acts 15:2)

'The whole assembly became silent as they listened to Barnabas and Paul telling about the signs and wonders God had done among the Gentiles through them.' (Acts 15:12)

I can just imagine these two men speaking courage into one another as they prepared to stand up and defend the gospel of grace. 'Come on, we can do this. God is with us. Don't be afraid. This is the grace of God we are defending. I'm with you heart and soul – let's do this!'

Courage is never the absence of fear, but the decision that there is something more important than fear at stake. Having people around you who can remind you of this, enables you to walk into situations you never thought you would be able to. Prophetic culture is always imbued with this 'can-do' spirit.

There have been so many situations where the encouragement

I needed to obey God came through the presence of courageous people by my side. On one occasion, we took my family for a day of outreach onto the streets in Bedford where we live. We have done this several times through the years, because mission should always be integrated into family life, not just a church programme.

Off we went into the town centre armed with a series of prophetic 'clues' as to the particular people we felt Jesus wanted to bless through us. Now, I am comfortable in many environments, but prophetic evangelism on the streets with people I do not know is certainly not one of them. I often melt with fear in such moments. My son and I loitered with intent around a store in town, waiting for someone who matched the descriptions God had given us. In particular we were looking for someone in a wheelchair.

Half hoping that no-one would show up so we could go home, we waited until a man pulled up outside the store in a wheelchair. It was precisely at that moment that I needed my courage buddy Sam, who instantly whispered loud enough for everyone to hear, 'There he is, Dad! Let's go!' Grabbing my arm and pulling me towards our 'treasure', the adventure was afoot. Having approached the man, who was now chatting to two ladies, he declined all of our offers for prayer saying he no longer trusted religion. Yet no sooner had he declined, one of the ladies said, 'Well, if he isn't going to have your prayers, perhaps I can?! Please will you pray for my daughter?'

As we started to pray, suddenly I began to get a prophetic download about many of the issues going on in her daughter's life. Specific situations, people, amounts of money and debts owed dropped into my mind as God began to unleash insight for that very moment. I began to pray over them each aspect of revelation God was showing me and, as I did, so their jaws began to drop and they began looking at one another in disbelief. I continued to pray prophetically God's solutions into her daughter's problems. It was a powerful moment of the Kingdom breaking in. As we finished praying, one of the ladies said, 'Are you a psychic or something? How on earth did you know all of those things?' A beautiful opportunity then opened to introduce Jesus to them – the one who is alive and speaks today.

Acts of Kingdom advance are sometimes just the other side of having people in your life who can speak courage to you. Without Sam, who was all of ten years old at the time, I may never have had the guts to take the plunge and obey God in that situation. Men and women of courageous obedience always write history. We all need a Barnabas in our life!

5. Make Space For Others to Shine

A hallmark of true greatness is the ability to make room for the strengths of other people, without feeling intimidated or threatened by them. Barnabas carried this hallmark. As soon as he finds Saul and brings him back to Antioch, he creates space for him to begin teaching the believers in the church. 'So for a whole year Barnabas and Saul met with the church and taught great numbers of people' (Acts 11:26).

So often, the unresolved control and insecurity issues of leaders reduce people, rather than empower them. If the success of other gifted people threatens your sense of significance or authority, you will always reduce people down to the level of your own dysfunction so that people remain 'under' you, rather than alongside you. The sad history of competition, jealousy and fear in churches through the years paints the very opposite picture of what Barnabas models to us.

Barnabas gives us a powerful demonstration of humility in action. The culture of encouragement he creates enables other people to play to their strengths. It is interesting to note that up until Acts 13:13 Barnabas is always mentioned first and Saul second. But after this point, the order switches as Doctor Luke, the writer of Acts, recognises that Paul (formerly Saul) has now become the primary team leader. Barnabas was big enough and secure enough to recognise when to make room and adjust his role in the team. He knew that Paul was destined to be the main apostolic culture shaper in the Gentile Church. How different history may have been, had Barnabas clung to his original position out of pride or fear.

I am convinced that one of the most important tasks of prophets is to help recognise emerging apostolic people and make them great. A number of years ago, when I was praying about where my family should relocate, God clearly spoke to me about moving to Bedford to be with my good friend Simon Holley. He said to me, 'Phil, you are not moving primarily for a place but to a person.' Instantly, I knew that one of God's great calls on my life was to serve and support Simon and add my strength to making him become all God has called him to as an apostle. My job is to lift him up, through prayer, encouragement and love. That's what prophets do. Don't let your own insecurities cloud your calling to create space for other people to shine.

In fact, it is Barnabas' incredible belief in people that eventually causes his pioneering partnership with Paul to end. A tragic split occurs between these two great leaders over their mutual friend John Mark.

'Some time later Paul said to Barnabas, "Let us go back and visit the believers in all the towns where we preached the word of the Lord and see how they are doing." Barnabas wanted to take John, also called Mark, with them, but Paul did not think it wise to take him, because he had deserted them in Pamphylia and had not continued with them in the work. They had such a sharp disagreement that they parted company.' (Acts 15:36-39)

So often the disagreements that divide us are not doctrinal but charismatic in nature. In other words, a failure to understand how our respective gifts operate can disable us from working fruitfully with one another. In this instance, Barnabas is doing what he has always done – encouraging the weak and believing in people, even those who have let him down. John Mark had deserted them in Pamphylia, yet Barnabas still believes the best and wants to draw greatness out of him, just as he had done with the apostle Paul a few chapters earlier.

Paul, however, is viewing the world through a different set of lenses. He is the pioneering apostle and evangelist focused on his mission to go to regions beyond with the gospel of Jesus Christ. Taking John Mark could potentially slow down or hinder the mission. The internal motivation of a culture shaper and innovator comes to the fore and clashes with the worldview of the encourager and pastoral prophet, Barnabas. They are looking at the same issue from two completely different gift perspectives and in the end it leads to a sad separation.

I wonder if they had known a little more about their respective strengths, whether they could have worked this one out? The enemy loves to turn the molehills of misunderstanding into mountains of misery. But the occasions where we see things differently can also be the very moments of creative tension God allows in order to bring breakthrough. Divinely held tension of different gifts is the fulcrum God uses to propel us into great Kingdom advance. We need each other. It is only in learning to recognise and honour what each of us carries that we truly can be more together than we are apart.

Prophetic cultures, because they are inherently encouraging environments, will always create space for people of different gifting and strength to rise to the surface. This will inevitably lead to moments of creative tension, as people who see the world differently rub shoulders with each other and have to make choices about how to define the terms of the relationship. Radical honour and authenticity are the two keys that enable diverse people and teams to play to one another's strengths, but also cover each other's weaknesses.

It's time for the sons and daughters of encouragement to step forward and shape the kind of world-changing cultures that propel God's people into the destiny designed by God for them. At the heart of the early Church was Barnabas, a man who created vibrant prophetic culture in his day. It really is this simple: encouragement changes lives and shapes nations.

Notes:

17. Strong's Concordance, http://biblehub.com/greek/3874.htm

18. http://www.abarim-publications.com/Meaning/Barnabas.html#.VuQ4psdiY3Q

Chapter Ten:
Changing the World Through Crazy Courage
Failure is an Option; Timidity is Not

I have been in church leadership for the best part of two decades, but I would never have had the courage to pursue God's calling on my life without a prophetic moment that changed me forever.

At the time, I was a teenager attending a large youth camp with my friends. Each evening, we would pile into a big-top tent to worship and hear teaching from the Bible. God was doing some extraordinary things in those days and one particular evening still stands out above all the rest. During one of the meetings, I was standing next to a good friend of mine. Another girl from our youth group approached him and simply shared that God wanted to say He really loved him. Instantaneously, as the words came out of her mouth, the power of the Spirit hit him and he fell backwards onto the floor, encountering God in a remarkable way.

What followed was life changing. For over four hours straight, my friend, who I had never heard prophesy before, began a continuous live-stream of prophetic revelation straight from the throne room. As he lay on his back on the grassy floor, he poured out all that God was showing him. Among many other things, he prophesied the collapse of communism in Europe, the breaking of the Berlin Wall, about Bibles being smuggled into China where a great revival would take place. Bear in mind that this happened in the late 1980s, before any of these events were world news. My friends and I were parked next to him, writing down every word he said.

Before I knew it, he started to prophesy about me too! Naming specific people, myself included, he prophesied God's calling to plant and lead churches in the UK. Instantly, I burst into tears and knew God had just given me my life's calling. It was a breathtaking encounter that has fed me ever since with the courage to do what God has asked me to do.

Genuine prophetic culture will always create an environment for men and women to live courageous lives. As we look into the pages of the New Testament, the prophetic so often released courage to believe God for extraordinary things, whether that was to provide financial help for those in famine, to send Barnabas and Saul on their first missionary journey or give Paul the courage to enter Jerusalem despite the persecution that awaited him (Acts 11:27-30; 13:1-3; 21:10-14). Let's consider together some of the ways the prophetic leads us to live lives of crazy courage.

1. Courage to Fail

One of the greatest obstacles to living a courageous life is the fear of failure. This crippling condition of the heart disables our forward momentum, because partnering with fear always leads to captivity or atrophy.

Earlier this year, as I was praying, God said to me, 'Phil, failure is an option, but timidity is not.' It made me reflect how often our fear of failure and need for performance-based approval drives whether we say 'yes' to God or not. But the way God defines success is so different from the way we do. We measure outcomes; God measures obedience. We are raised to believe that failure is bad, but in the Kingdom, there is no growth without heroic failure!

I have a good friend who wanted to grow in his prophetic evangelism skills, especially giving words of knowledge on the streets so he could share the gospel more effectively. Deciding the only way to grow was to have a go, he took himself off to a local park where he saw a man sitting by himself on a bench. Asking God for some revelation about this man, he felt God say, 'The man's name is Maurice.' Armed with this information, my friend sauntered over and casually sat down next to the gentleman in question and struck up a conversation. 'Nice weather today isn't it . . . Maurice?' The man looked at my friend with a rather strange and quizzical expression but grunted a reply. Undeterred, my friend followed up with several more questions, each time slipping in the name 'Maurice' for added effect. Finally, the man turned to my friend and said, 'Listen, why do you keep calling me Maurice? My name's Dave – clear off!'

Heroic failures like this, while funny, are actually very inspiring. The reality is, to grow we need to have a go and those who criticise from the sidelines never write history. Prophetic cultures are characterised by their ability to nurture a 'can-do' spirit, in which the saints regularly ask each other, 'What is God saying to you and what are you going to do about it?'

Every year, during annual appraisals, Craig Groeschel, a pastor in the US, asks his staff team, 'What one thing have you tried this year that has failed?' If the staff team member is unable to point to an area where they courageously gave something a go and it didn't quite work out, they get a sound rebuke![19]

As soon as our reward comes from outcome rather than obedience, we have capped any potential for Kingdom growth in or through us, because growth always requires trial and error. You cannot control your way to increase. Increase only comes from co-operation with the Holy Spirit. My highest reward has to come from saying yes to Him. Failure is not just an option; it is an absolute necessity.

As soon as your reputation exceeds your risk taking, you have decided how far you are able to grow. So often we stop taking risks because we believe, falsely, that if we fail it ruins any credibility we have already developed. Not only is this thinking rooted in fear of man, it chronically limits what God is able to do through us. Part of a leader's responsibility is to demonstrate how to fail well!

Paul writes to the sometimes fear-prone Timothy, saying, 'For God has not given us a spirit of fear and timidity, but of power, love, and self-discipline' (2 Timothy 1:7 NLT). Paul is reminding Timothy that his new identity in Christ did not come pre-packaged with fear, but instead with the Jesus-like qualities of courage, power, love and self-discipline. This is who you now are. Fear is an illegal imposter, masquerading as your friend. You have a new reality to your life. You are a man or woman of prophetic courage. You were born to change the world. You have been fashioned by your Father to be like the ultimate man of courage, Jesus.

Conrad Humphreys is a record-breaking yachtsman, known for his daring deeds on the high seas. His preparation process for one specific solo race, the Transat,[20] involved training himself, a whole year in advance of the expedition, to survive on less than 20 minutes of sleep at a time in order to cope with the horrendous sleep deprivation ahead. Chronic fatigue regularly plagues ocean racers and induces some strange side-effects. Sure enough, on the gruelling trip itself, he began to hallucinate. Weary from days without sleep, Humphreys imagined the actress Jennifer Aniston had joined him on deck. She promptly told him to go downstairs and get some sleep and that she would take charge.

Relieved to have some help, Humphreys went below, completely undressed and snuggled down for some well-earned rest. He was rudely awakened a few hours later by the sound of a mid-Atlantic gale and his rigging screaming in the wind. Realising Jennifer had only been a figment of his imagination, he ran onto deck to find parts of his boat flying off and breaking in the storm. Staring death in the face, his one thought in that moment was, 'What if they find my body and wonder why I am completely naked!'

Asked by reporters why he put himself through such rigours, Humphreys simply replied, 'Facing your fears is where the life really is!'

If you are living a life that requires no courage, you are not really living. To live as a Christian at school, to share your faith, to love the unlovable, to develop a prayer life, to live with purity, to pioneer a business, to love your neighbour – these things take great courage. Any old Joe can go with the flow, but it takes guts to live the Jesus way. Timidity is just no longer an option. What would you do if you had no fear of failure?

2. The Courage to Say a Bigger 'Yes'
The presence of the prophetic in our lives should inspire us to say 'yes' to Jesus. As the people of God, recently returned from exile, began to rebuild the temple, they were given courage to say a bigger 'yes' because of prophetic influence in their culture.

'So the elders of the Jews built and prospered, through the prophesying of the prophet Haggai and Zechariah son of Iddo. They finished their building by command of the God of Israel and by decree of Cyrus, Darius, and King Artaxerxes of Persia'. (Ezra 6:14 NRSV)

Haggai and Zechariah inspire an ongoing ability to say 'yes' to the work of rebuilding the ancient ruins in Jerusalem. Many times through the years the prophetic has been characterised by what is has been against and what it says 'no' to. The truth is, sometimes the best 'no' is a bigger 'yes' to something much more worthwhile and eternal. The prophetic creates courage to say 'yes' to God in increasing measure. You are always growing in God. One simple measure of spiritual maturity is this: is my 'yes' to God getting bigger than my 'no'?

Queen Victoria once summoned the great pioneer and founder of the Salvation Army, William Booth. It is said that Booth was late for his appointment because he refused Her Majesty's offer of a carriage, remarking, 'If the poor of London have to walk, so shall I.' Having arrived, the Queen asked Booth, 'What is the secret of your ministry? How is it that others are so pale, so pallid, so powerless, so weak and you are so mighty?'

Apparently Booth took a piece of chalk from his pocket and drew a circle on the palace floor. Stepping inside it, and with tears streaming down his cheeks, he told Queen Victoria, 'Everything inside this circle belongs wholly to God. Your majesty, I guess the reason is because God has all there is of me . . . God knows I am hungering to keep souls out of hell.'[21]

How much of you is inside the circle? We sometimes mistakenly believe that courage is the absence of anxiety or fear. Actually, true courage is the decision that there is something more important at stake than my fears. Courage is not an emotion but a decision, fuelled by love for a person. Jesus.

Prophets, like Booth, create a holy appetite for saying 'yes' in the people of God. They do this through words, inspiration, friendship, encouragement, preaching, correcting, empowering and, most of all, through example.

A good prophetic friend of mine was out in the city centre on a busy Saturday shopping day. He had just finished a session of healing on the streets,[22] a ministry model of seeing God's power bring breakthrough for those who are sick or in pain. A group of teenagers had been standing at the edge of proceedings, watching with thinly veiled interest. As the team were packing up to go, two of them approached my friend and asked what was going on. He told them that they had been praying for sickness to leave in Jesus' name and asked if either of them had anything they wanted prayer for. One of the young men replied, 'I've got no ligaments in either of my thumbs,' and promptly demonstrated the fact by bending back both appendages in an unearthly manner.

'Right, let's pray. In fact, why don't you invite all your friends to come and see what God is about to do as well?' my friend boldly asked. Starting with one thumb at a time, he prayed and watched as God's power worked an astonishing miracle before their eyes. Now when the young man tried to bend his thumbs back, as he had done before, he was unable to. God had grown ligaments in an instant to the utter shock of all those watching. That group of teenagers then had a very personal encounter with the King as my friend prayed for them each in turn, and God began to meet with them. They would not forget this occasion in a hurry!

Mel Gibson, playing the famous Scottish leader William Wallace in the film *Braveheart*, says, 'Men don't follow titles, they follow courage.'[23] Prophetic cultures do not promote conservative conformity to religious norms but courageous collaboration with the Holy Spirit. It's time to say 'yes' and watch what He does with our faith-filled obedience.

3. The Courage to Break Barriers

As Joshua stood on the cusp of entering the long-awaited Promised Land, he faced a new challenge. To get to where he had never been would require him to do something that had never been done. Breaking barriers requires great courage. What Joshua hears from the Lord in that very moment comes as no surprise:

'Be strong and courageous, because you will lead these people to inherit the land I swore to their ancestors to give them. Be strong and very courageous. Be careful to obey all the law my servant Moses gave you; do not turn from it to the right or to the left, that you may be successful wherever you go.'
(Joshua 1:6-7)

Joshua was called to lead Israel into totally unchartered waters and it was prophetic revelation directly from God that enabled him to swim there. Prophetic culture is filled with the belief that

God's people are not merely meant to survive, but thrive, as they bring about the invasion of His Kingdom in unprecedented ways.

One of the reasons God places prophets in the Church is to help the people of God believe they have been made to change the world. Prophets lift our sights above our current circumstances and fix them upon heavenly aspirations birthed in the unseen realms of God's glory and wisdom. Joshua was going to do what had never been done before and the courage he needed to go there came through hearing the voice of the Lord.

Innovation always requires extraordinary courage. Joshua was about to innovate the first ever fortified wall demolition using nothing but a marching band and the blowing of trumpets. This God-given strategy did not come from an established military manual or tried and tested methodology. It was impossible. But that is exactly what hearing God's voice enables us to do. The impossible becomes the new norm of believers caught up in God's prophetic purposes.

Years ago, I sat drinking coffee in an English hotel with a good friend as he began to share with me the growing sense of prophetic burden God was giving him for the poor. At the time he was working in a successful marketing firm but could not shake the sense that God was calling him to break down barriers and help some of the most marginalised in our society. Something prophetic had gripped his heart and every time we met together in subsequent months the longing to pour out his life in compassion grew stronger.

My main role in those days was simply to speak courage into his heart. 'You can do this! God is with you. He will provide. You can trust Him. Go for it!' Facing the uncertain prospect of how he would provide for his family and where these new God-dreams would lead him, my friend courageously took the plunge, left his job and set out on a new adventure, not knowing where it would all end up.

During the first year of this scary adventure, unpaid and trusting God to provide, he carried out research into the biggest needs in Newcastle upon Tyne and came out with one answer. Destitution. More specifically, the destitution that was being experienced by hundreds of asylum seekers and refugees in the city. The front cover of his subsequent report, 'Destitute and Desperate', featured an Iranian asylum-seeker, Abas Amini, who went on hunger strike and sewed his own eyes and mouth together in opposition to the British Home Office's decision to turn down his appeal to stay in the UK. It painted a graphic picture of the plight of some of the most vulnerable people in the nation. This was an area that few people or organisations wanted to fund, was politically unpopular and faced huge obstacles. Welcome to your calling!

Ten years on, he has established an impressive award-winning charity called 'Action Foundation',[24] which is successfully tackling some of the key exclusion issues experienced by asylum seekers and refugees in the north-east of England. Hundreds of the most vulnerable people in our society have been rescued and supported, through housing, language schools, advocacy and friendship. His courage to pursue God's prophetic calling has released extraordinary hope. Breaking barriers takes courage, but that is exactly what you and I are called to do.

The Church today is not called to copy-cat the anointing and breakthroughs of previous generations. While they can inspire and teach us a great deal, the only real power comes from obeying the voice of Jesus. That alone equips us to innovate and break barriers in our day.

Facing the Giants
One of the reasons the prophetic is so important when we start to embrace our call to break barriers is that, without it, it is so easy to give up. Innovating and bringing about positive change is

a difficult business. God's words enable us to fight and keep going (1 Timothy 1:18). Creating environments where we hear God's voice clearly enables us to steer our course by what God has said, not what critics throw at us.

Almost every innovation in history is preceded by great criticism and opposition, often from those perceived as experts in the area in question. Just take a look at the following examples:

'This telephone has too many shortcomings to be seriously considered as a means of communication. The device is inherently of no value to us.' Western Union internal memo, 1876

'Man will never reach the moon regardless of all future scientific advances.' Dr Lee Defrost, father of radio and grandfather of television.

'I think there is a world market for maybe five computers.' Thomas Watson, chairman of IBM 1943

'We don't like their sound, and guitar music is on the way out.' Decca Recording Studios, rejecting The Beatles in 1962.

'Airplanes are interesting toys but of no military value.' Marceal Ferdinand Foch, professor of strategy France.[25]

What these examples reveal, is that those who steward yesterday's innovations often oppose tomorrow's breakthroughs. In an effort to preserve what we already have, we cease to sow into what we need in the future. Spiritual famine is so often the product of misused wealth. The apostle Paul lays down this vital spiritual principle when he says, 'Now he who supplies seed to the sower and bread for food will also supply and increase your store of seed and will enlarge the harvest of your righteousness. You will be enriched in every way so that you can be generous on every occasion, and through us your generosity will result in thanksgiving to God' (2 Corinthians 9:10-11).

God always gives you bread and seed: something to enjoy today and something to invest in tomorrow. When God blesses us, be that with finances, homes, friendships, ideas, courage, energy or talents, it is always part of His investment plan for the future. As we give, we experience God enlarging our harvest of righteousness. This is a vital spiritual principle.

Because the enemy of our souls hates the expansion of the Kingdom, he will do whatever he can, by whatever means necessary, to stop you from advancing into your future. Before every breakthrough there is a battle.

God has enlisted His people into the great business of extending the rule of Christ across the whole planet. We should expect to encounter opposition along the way. When we do, we don't fight aimlessly, but with the great and precious promises of God in our mouths and minds.

God's promises enable us to stare down the fear-inducing schemes of the enemy that attempt to stop us from advancing. Most people never cross into their promised land like Joshua because they allow fear to dictate the boundaries of their future. We reduce our lives to accommodate the giants, and mistake the silence for peace.

You and I have to go through giants and Jericho walls to get to the Promised Land. You were born to break barriers. That's who you now are.

4. Courage Flows from Someone
On the eve of conquering Jericho, Joshua has an encounter with the pre-incarnate Jesus (Joshua 5:13-15). This 'Commander of the armies of the Lord' invades Joshua's world and swallows up

his fear through a holy moment of awe and wonder.

Joshua's courage did not flow from something, it flowed from someone. The answer for living a courageous life is to become more impressed by someone else, than by yourself!

The apostle John spells out the very essence of the prophetic when he writes: 'For the testimony of Jesus is the spirit of prophecy' (Revelation 19:10 NRSV). This is so crucial. Prophetic cultures will always encourage people into an encounter and love relationship with Jesus. He is the focal point of attention, adoration and worship. Jesus is the one from whom all life flows.

'The Son is the image of the invisible God, the firstborn over all creation. For in him all things were created: things in heaven and on earth, visible and invisible, whether thrones or powers or rulers or authorities; all things have been created through him and for him. He is before all things, and in him all things hold together. And he is the head of the body, the church; he is the beginning and the firstborn from among the dead, so that in everything he might have the supremacy. For God was pleased to have all his fullness dwell in him, and through him to reconcile to himself all things, whether things on earth or things in heaven, by making peace through his blood, shed on the cross.' (Colossians 1:15-20)

Knowing Jesus is the focal point of every prophetic culture and genuine courage only flows from encountering Him. When Paul prays that the Ephesians 'know the love of Christ that surpasses knowledge' (Ephesians 3:19 NRSV) he does not have in mind a purely academic gathering of more information. The 'knowing' used here speaks of knowledge through personal first-hand experience.[26] It is the same word used of the Virgin Mary when she says to the angel, 'How will this be since I do not know a man?' (Luke 1:34 NRSV).

Knowing Christ experientially is the obsession of genuine prophetic cultures. For this reason, the prophetic will always be pushing us to go deeper into the presence of God and an experience of Jesus' glory. Life flows from knowing Christ, through first-hand encounter. When Jesus defines the nature of eternity, He does so in these words, 'Now this is eternal life: that they know you, the only true God, and Jesus Christ, whom you have sent' (John 17:3).

Knowing Jesus is not the route to something greater. It is, itself, the greater thing. The parameters of eternity are defined by this great and central calling – to know Him, just as I am fully known. Knowing Jesus is the source of courage, because when you truly see Him, your fears seem less and less plausible. This is what has enabled Christian martyrs through the centuries to face death without shrinking back. Knowing Christ!

I was privileged to watch video footage of a group of Romanian teenagers worshipping, lost in adoration and wonder as they loved Jesus together. Without them realising, as the footage continued to play, the room slowly began to fill with a mist followed by thick cloud, to the point where you could hardly see them any more. The glory of the Lord's presence had come in a manifest way. The pastor who was showing the film told me that at the very same moment, in another part of the camp, teenagers who did not yet know Jesus spontaneously began to seek Him and give their lives to Him.

We have the privilege of pursuing and standing in the presence of God today, because we have been hardwired to live in the presence of His glory for all eternity. In His glory, the miraculous becomes effortless and the supernatural normal. Prioritising knowing Jesus experientially means leaving lots of space for glory moments, where there is no agenda other than enjoying Him. Where is that happening in your life, your family or your church? Prophetic cultures create space to know God personally, because there is no greater thing.

Conclusion

I believe God is raising up the most courageous generation the world has ever seen and only history will tell how much of us we put inside the circle. I am convinced that God is more interested in making our lives meaningful than He is making them comfortable. You were not saved to sit on the sidelines and spectate, but to get on the pitch and participate. Prophetic culture, by its very nature, will raise sons and daughters who dare to dream and who consider anything possible for those who believe. This is not a time to hold back. It is a time to advance in the strength God gives.

Your courage to change the world can only come from one person. Jesus. And He is the best last word a book on prophetic culture could or should ever have.

Jesus.

Notes:

19. Graig Groeschel, *IT: How Churches and Leaders Can Get It and Keep It*, Zondervan.

20. http://www.independent.co.uk/sport/general/sailing-humphreys-ready-for-ocean-ordeal-with-help-from-imaginary-friends-18885.html

21. Fred M. Barlow, 2000, *Profiles in Evangelism*, Sword of the Lord Publishers, p31.

22. http://www.healingonthestreets.com/mark-marx/

23. http://www.imdb.com/title/tt0112573/quotes

24. http://www.actionfoundation.org.uk/downloads/Destitute%20and%20Desperate.pdf

25. http://www.actionfoundation.org.uk

26. http://web.mit.edu/randy/www/words.html

27. http://strongsnumbers.com/greek/1097.htm